THE Physics OF HEAVEN

Exploring God's Mysteries of Sound, Light, Energy, Vibrations, and Quantum Physics

By Judy Franklin and Ellyn Davis

©2012 Judy Franklin & Ellyn Davis

All rights reserved. This book is protected by the copyright laws of the United States of America. No part of this publication may be reproduced, distributed, or transmitted in any form or by any means, or stored in a database or retrieval system without the prior written permission of the publisher.

In chapters where others are quoted, copyright guidelines concerning the "fair use" of material have been observed and no explicit permission for reprinted quotes is necessary. In chapters extracted from interviews or writings of others, permission has been given by that author or author's publisher to use excerpts of their interviews or writings in this book. Unless otherwise noted, Scripture quotations are from the New King James Version, Copyright © 1992 by Thomas Nelson Publishers. Used by permission of Thomas Nelson Publishers. All rights reserved.

ISBN-10: 0983309728
ISBN-13: 978-0-9833097-2-7
DPP Double Portion Publishing
1053 Eldridge Loop
Crossville, TN 38571
www.doubleportionpublishing.com
Specializing in helping authors self-publish their books.

Cover design by Blake Davis at *www.cblakedavis.com*
Excerpting and editing of contributor material by Ellyn Davis
Layout, formatting and page design by Ellyn Davis

Acknowledgements

We want to extend a special thank you to each of the contributors for your time and wonderful insights: Bob Jones, Bill Johnson, Jonathan Welton, Ray Hughes, Cal Pierce, Dan McCollam, Larry Randolph, Beni Johnson, and David Van Koevering. It was truly an honor to have you contribute to this work.

Thank you Ray Hughes for granting permission to print excerpts from your book; and Dan McCollam for allowing us to print excerpts of your unpublished manuscript. We also appreciate Destiny Image's permission to reprint excerpts from books by Bill Johnson and Jonathan Welton.

Many thanks also to Jordan Schilperoort, James Schoensiegel, Heather Ridnour and Julie Mustard for their editorial help and encouragement. Thank you Kendra Wieck, for your help transcribing the countless hours of contributor interviews. And thanks to Blake Davis for editorial help and for designing the cover of the book.

Thank you, Randall Worley, for believing in the project and encouraging us to follow through with it. And thank you Jerry Aaronson, for your inspiring presentation on sound that helped us finalize the structure of this book.

Please note: The contents of this book are based on interviews and research conducted by the authors and contributors as well as on their life experiences. The publisher and authors present this information for inspirational and educational purposes only. Therefore, the reader should be aware that this information is not intended as spiritual advice, doctrinal position, or comprehensive scientific fact, but rather is intended to be a sharing of knowledge and information from the research and experience of the authors and contributors. The publisher and authors encourage you, the reader, to thoroughly investigate and prayerfully consider for yourself the topics introduced in this book and come to your own conclusions about them.

Endorsements

As I began reading this book I felt a great sense of excitement well up within my spirit. Of course there is an amazing convergence between the insights of quantum physics and biblical revelation! Those of us who have embraced the revelation of God recognise that the natural world is a source of great revelatory insight into the handiwork of our awesome Creator. But until recently, exploration of the convergence of science and spirituality has been almost exclusively dominated by New Age metaphysics. A handful of progressive evangelical authors have noted the convergence between science and spirituality but virtually nothing has been written in this field by charismatic Christians who are fully switched on to the present reality of the supernatural inbreaking of the kingdom of heaven. That is why this book excites me. I strongly encourage you to dig deep into this compilation of prophetic insights into the collision between heaven and earth and our strategic role in releasing the glory of God here on earth.

Phil Mason

Spiritual Director, New Earth Tribe, Byron Bay, Australia

Author, ***Quantum Glory: The Science of Heaven Invading Earth***

In a world where there are many voices vying to direct our attention to different things, God has raised up Judy Franklin and Ellyn Davis to be a voice that leads people to encounter God in a fresh and significant way. *The Physics of Heaven* is yet another shining example of Judy's and Ellyn's passion to see people encounter Jesus. Even as they tackle the complex topics of sound, light, vibrations, and quantum physics, they call people to a deeper and more intimate relationship with Him. However, this is nothing new since their life is an inspiring example in the Body of Christ leading people to expand their horizons and experience the extravagance of God in a new way.

Banning Liebscher
Jesus Culture Director
Bethel Church in Redding, California

Judy and Ellyn are prophetic adventurers on the edges of kingdom understanding, ahead of their time, exploring realms untouched by many Christians. I love their heart of exploration and curiosity that has been previously reserved for Christian mystics of past centuries. *The Physics of Heaven* will awaken a child like curiosity that will draw you beyond the veil of personal limitation, and into a heavenly expedition you may have never experienced before. Enjoy the journey!

Steve Witt
Senior Leader, Bethel Church, Cleveland

Contents

Foreword by Kris Vallotton i
Introduction: A Glimpse of Things to Come v
A Habitation of Dragons xiii

Chapters

1 The Power of the Zero Point Field—*Judy Franklin* 1
  Dolphin Therapy 10
2 Extracting the Precious—*Ellyn Davis* 11
  Squeamish Yet? 20
3 Vibrating in Harmony With God—*Bob Jones* 21
  Healing Energy 28
4 Recovering Spiritual Inheritance—*Bill Johnson* 29
  Healing Hands 40
5 Authentic versus Counterfeit—*Jonathan Welton* 41
  God's New Sound is Coming 52
6 Good Vibrations—*Ellyn Davis* 53
  Brainwaves 64
7 Sound of Heaven—*Ray Hughes* 65
  Power of Sound 76
8 The God Vibration—*Dan McCollam* 77

Cymatics 87

9 Angelic Encounters—*Cal Pierce* 89

   The Schumann Resonance 94

10 Spiritual Synesthesia—*Larry Randolph* 95

   Synesthesia 107

   Music and the Near Death Experience 108

11 Strange Things are Afoot—*Ellyn Davis* 109

   Solfeggio Frequencies 120

12 Quantum Mysticism—*Ellyn Davis* 121

   The Power of Color 132

13 Your Quantum Leap—*David Van Koevering* 133

   Popping Qwiffs 145

   Mind Over Matter 146

14 Whole Lotta Shaking Going On 147

   Your Body is an Electromagnetic Field 160

   Sensing Magnetic Fields 162

15 The Clarion Call—*Beni Johnson* 163

   Human Body Frequencies 170

16 Pulling Into Today—*Bill Johnson* 171

About the Authors 181
Recommended Resources 186
Contact Information 187

Foreword
by Kris Vallotton

In this powerful book, Judy Franklin and Ellyn Davis assemble a team of seers who peer behind the curtain of creation to reveal the mysterious nature of our Creator. This book reads like a journal that emerged from a Holy Spirit think tank where great, spiritual leaders gathered to discuss their insights into the complexities of God. Through their collective intelligence these seers have emerged with new perspectives never before pondered.

This book is a foretaste of things to come, unearthing what the great Apostle Paul penned nearly two thousand years ago. "Since the creation of the world God's invisible attributes, His eternal power and divine nature, have been clearly seen, being understood through what has been made..." (Romans 1:20). What a profound revelation! Creation itself is like heavenly breadcrumbs strategically placed on the path of life to lead us into understanding the depths of God.

The Apostle Paul went on to say that the Saints are to,"...bring to light...the mystery which for ages has been hidden in God who created all things; so that the manifold wisdom

Foreword

of God might now be made known through the church to the rulers and the authorities in the heavenly places," (Ephesians 3:8-9).

I love the fact that *The Physics of Heaven*, isn't written by scientists trying to discover the nature of God through some intellectual pursuit. Nor is it a philosophical monologue subjugated to rational and logical thinking reducing God to the laws of physics. Instead these authors have set out on a journey into the very foundations of creation with the Holy Spirit as their instructor, mentor and tour guide.

This unique approach to science results in multidimensional perspectives that very well could be the beginning of this Ephesians passage being unveiled to spiritual beings in heavenly places.

The Physics of Heaven is not the final word on creation's revelation of God, nor is it a treasure map that leads to a specific truth that unlocks nature's secrets. It's more like a divine invitation to join these supernatural explorers, who like Columbus before them, refuse to believe that the world is flat. Leaving the safe haven of conventional thinking, they set sail in uncharted waters with a passion to discover new lands.

Like highly skilled sailors, hand-picked for a treacherous expedition, each of these authors masterfully record their personal insights, which leads to a beautiful collage of unfolding wisdom.

If you are tired of being a settler, existing on the shores of tradition and riskless living, this book is for you. But

Foreword

beware, because once you get a taste of these authors' insights into light, sound, vibration and quantum physics and you discover how God has written His personal story into creation, you are destined to see the Almighty all around you. Like listening to surround sound while watching a great movie, this book will awaken nature's voice in you, curing deafness that was predicated long ago by single dimensional thinking.

The whistle is blowing and it's time to set sail into the great adventure. Won't you join us?

Kris Vallotton
Senior Associate Leader of Bethel Church, Redding, CA
Author of *The Supernatural Ways of Royalty* and *Spirit Wars*

There are things that we know we know. There are things that are unknown that we know we don't know. But there are also things that are unknown that we don't know we don't know. These "unknown unknowns" limit our ability to foresee what is coming because they create in us a poverty of expectations.

Introduction
A Glimpse of Things to Come

My journey into the mysteries of sound, light, vibrations, and quantum physics began with one word—"sound."

In 1999, during one of my quiet times with the Lord, He mentioned the word "sound." Nothing more, just a word—"sound." There was nothing unusual about this, because God often speaks just one word or one sentence to me and I may not hear more from Him about that word or phrase for quite a while.

When He spoke the word "sound," I began reading all I could on the topic. At that time, several very well known prophets began sharing what they felt they were hearing from God about sound. But once I researched as much as I could, I began losing interest because I didn't know what to do with what I was learning. After awhile, I began to realize it was like God was playing a game with me.

This is how He would play this game. Sometimes He would say a word—just one word like the word "sound"— and then would be silent. I would then look up the word in the Bible, both Greek and Hebrew. I would read the references to it. I would find the definition in the dictionary. I would ask Him

Introduction

about the word. Through this, He would show me wonderful things connected to that word.

At other times, I would be reading a book or magazine or watching a movie and something would stand out to me, and I'd know it was a "hint" of something greater. What I was watching or reading didn't have to be Christian, it just had to have something in it that "spoke" to me, like when God spoke the word "sound."

I called this "game" the "How badly do you want it?" game because it was like God was giving me a piece of a puzzle He wanted me to put together. But it took effort to keep searching because it would often be a long time before I found the next piece. That's what happened when He spoke the word "sound" to me. I would find a piece, and, just when I had almost forgotten about the puzzle, God would tell me something new or show me something different about sound and off I would go, doing more research. But I had no idea how the insights and information I was discovering would ever fit together.

In December, 2010, when Ellyn and I first discussed writing this book together, we were so excited. After all, for years, each of us had been collecting information and insights and gathering our own puzzle pieces. So, we thought we could easily get the book written and published in just a few months. But nothing worked the way we thought it would. The book has taken us over a year to write and there are still a number of things we had to leave out because there just wasn't room to share everything we've been researching and discovering.

Introduction

This book is a conglomeration of the things Ellyn and I have learned about sound, light, energy, frequencies, vibrations, and quantum physics. It also shares insights God has shown others. None of the people who have written chapters or given interviews could be considered an expert in quantum physics or any of the other subjects covered in the book. We all simply share what the Lord has been revealing to us.

First the Natural

First Corinthians 15: 46 says, "...the spiritual is not first, but the natural; then the spiritual." We believe that there's a lot we can learn about God by looking at the natural world. Jesus used parables about nature and natural processes like sheep and grapes and weather and growing crops to describe the spiritual. We believe that God is revealing things in the sciences, particularly in quantum physics, that can be directly related to the spiritual realm.

The revelatory connection between quantum physics and the spirit realm poses an uncomfortable challenge. Christianity has traditionally rejected much of what scientists propose because their conclusions haven't necessarily been drawn from a biblical world view. We like science when it makes discoveries that improve our health or lifestyle, but we are uncomfortable when it comes to entertaining some of the ideas scientists have drawn from quantum physics.

As I said, this book is a conglomeration of different insights and information gleaned by Ellyn, me, and the other contributors. Its sole purpose is to share what we have dis-

Introduction

covered so you can go on your own journey of discovery with God into the realms of sound, light, energy, vibration, and quantum physics. Why? Because I believe what the Lord has been showing both of us is the absolute truth that will help us bring God's kingdom to this earth. The Lord is ready to use sound, light, and energy in ways we never dreamed, but we first need to have some foundational understandings.

A Word From God

Here is a prophetic word the Lord gave me about the coming importance of sound.

> *Just as the people were in the upper room on the day of Pentecost, when suddenly there came from heaven a noise, and this noise was like a violent rushing wind, there will come again a noise that I will release from heaven. This noise—this sound—will be released and, just as those people in that upper room were changed, people who hear this sound that I will release will be changed. While I am not calling any of my people to sit in an upper room and wait, I am calling them to a place where their spirits are in an upper room position to receive what I am about to release. This sound that I will release will cause people to think differently.*

Visions

After I had researched sound for nearly 10 years, the Lord began showing me visions of what was to come. This re-

Introduction

ally excited me and I began sharing what God was showing me wherever I went. The visions are like movies and they take place after God has released His new sound and people are transformed by it.

In one of the movies, I saw Christians who had been affected by the coming God sound standing on the shore of an island like Japan. A tsunami was coming and as it approached the shore, all they did was point to the tsunami and command it to stop and suddenly everything became still.

In other visions I saw Christians who had been transformed by God's sound stopping floods and natural disasters. I saw hurricanes headed towards our coast and Christians speaking to the winds and telling them to stop. The winds obeyed and everything became calm. I saw tornadoes moving towards a town and the people who were affected by this new sound pointed at the tornadoes and told them to stop and the whirlwinds collapsed into nothing. I saw people who were changed by the sound God is going to release watching a wildfire so out of control nothing could put it out. These Christians pointed to the fire and told it to stop and it was immediately extinguished.

I also saw believers so in love with God and so filled with power after being changed by this sound that unbelievers would run to them begging to receive what they have. I saw the greatest revival the world has ever known, filled with people clamoring to know this magnificent God of ours.

I saw us walking in such love and power that the world could no longer deny that there is a God, that He sent His son Jesus so that we might know Him, and that He gave us

Introduction

His Holy Spirit to empower us to do the work He has called us to do.

About the Book

This book is just a precursor to the revelation that God is going to give us when He releases a new, transforming sound. In the first section, Ellyn and I share our journey of discovery about sound, light, vibrations, energy, and quantum physics. Bill Johnson writes that we can't just camp around old truth, but should seek newly revealed truths for our generation and then preserve those truths for the generations that follow.

And then, because we are exploring territory that some people fear is full of counterfeits, Jonathan Welton explains that Christians need not be afraid of being deceived by counterfeits, but should realize that whenever we see a counterfeit, we should try to discover the "real" behind it.

You will learn about sound in all of its forms. You'll read what some astrophysicists have to say about energy, light, power, and frequencies. You'll find testimonies of how sound has affected people in the past and how it is affecting people today. And you will learn what many Christian leaders are sensing and hearing from God about sound, light, energy, and vibrations.

This book is not a definitive scientific work on the topics it covers. It was never intended to be. It is more of a composite of the puzzle pieces we've found so far. We wanted to share them with you so you could start praying about this "new sound from God" and meditating on God's word whenever He

Introduction

shows you something about sound, keeping your heart in an upper room position to receive all God has for all of us.

I've read the end of the book called the Bible, and guess what? We win! God said he would never forsake us, so to me the greatest error we could ever commit is to think that this world is going to get so bad that He will snatch us out quickly before we all die. That is not winning. That is not showing the world who He is; a wonderful, loving, kind God who is eager to save. It is also not showing the world how powerful we are because God has given us His power. We have not even yet begun to experience all that God wants us to do and to be.

So read on with an open heart, engage your mind, and believe God for a new, transforming sound.

Judy Franklin
May 1, 2012

P.S. Ellyn and I would love to hear what the Lord is telling you concerning the topics covered in this book. Please share with us at the book's website: *www.heavensphysics.com.*

The veil between the earthly realm and the heavenly realm is thinner than ever. Ask the Spirit of God to open your eyes to behold the realm of the spirit. The strange dissatisfaction you feel is your spirit hungering and thirsting for God.

—Bobby Conner

A Habitation of Dragons

Many years ago, ancient maps showed the extent of the known world. At the edge of the maps was unknown territory, usually depicted by tempest-tossed seas filled with monsters and dragons. This "habitation of dragons" was considered too dangerous to enter because there was no way to know what you might find out there and there was always the possibility that, once you went beyond the horizon of the familiar, you would never return.

Eventually explorers such as Cortez, Magellan, Balboa and Columbus decided to test the waters. All of them were convinced there were valuable discoveries out where everyone thought the dragons lived and they were willing to do whatever it took to find new lands, bring back their riches, and lead future generations to them.

This is the way it is with all unknowns. First, there are explorers willing to test the waters and see if there really arc dragons there and hopefully find never-before-seen riches. Then there are pioneers who follow in the footsteps of the explorers and are the first to settle the new lands. Finally, once the new territory is considered dragon-free, settlers arrive and build cities.

Others have gone before us and explored the things we write about in this book, but we are both on our own voyage of discovery into new territory and want to share with you what we've found so far.

We think of this book as kind of an archipelago* of discoveries, with each thought or wondering an "island." Maybe you don't want to visit every island and maybe some "islands" of insight and information are more interesting to you than others. Maybe some islands are downright scary to explore. That's OK.

We invite you to come along with us on our voyage of discovery into unmapped territory. Take the tour of the "islands" we've explored and maybe even discover some of your own that we've overlooked.

Judy and Ellyn

*archipelago—a sea or stretch of water containing many islands

1

The Power of the Zero-Point Field
by Judy Franklin

*H*ave you ever read a passage in the Bible and found yourself coming back to it again and again? It's like there is something in those particular verses that somehow latches onto your spirit and you just have to understand what they mean.

That's the way it was with me several years ago when I read Romans 8:18 - 22.

> *For I consider that the sufferings of this present time are not worthy to be compared with the glory that is to be revealed to us. For the anxious longing of the creation waits eagerly for the revealing of the sons of God. For the creation was subjected to futility, not willingly, but because of Him who subjected it, in hope that the creation itself also will be set free from its slavery to corruption into the freedom of the glory of the children of God. For we know that the whole creation groans and suffers the pains of childbirth together until now.*

What exactly does Paul mean when he says that all of creation is held back, longing, waiting, groaning, and travailing until the children of God are revealed? Hadn't the children of God already been revealed by the time Paul wrote this letter to the Romans? After all, this was years after Jesus' crucifixion and resurrection, years after Pentecost, and even years after followers of Jesus were called "Christians" and "the men who turned the world upside down." According to the book of Acts, miracles and healings and deliverances and even resurrections from the dead were almost commonplace. So what exactly was Paul talking about? What is the "manifestation" or "revealing" of the children of God?

I felt like there was more to those verses so I began earnestly seeking the Lord as to what they meant. He shared that, from the day of Pentecost until now, no child of God has ever fully realized the power that has been put within us. God has given us power to raise the dead and heal the sick and cast out demons and we've done that to a point, but....

Although we are extremely happy and grateful for the power we have operated in, it in no way has reached the measure of what He intends for us. Jesus said that we would do greater works than He did, but no Christian in history has exceeded Jesus' works.

The next thing the Lord told me was that soon He would release a sound from heaven that will literally change the structure of how we think. This new sound will transform us like the transformation spoken of in Romans 12. Our minds will be renewed so that we think like Him and are no longer conformed to this world but conformed to the will of God. Bringing heaven to earth is our mandate, and to do that we need to think more like heaven.

The Zero-Point Field

I began thinking about the day of Pentecost. One hundred and twenty believers were in an upper room in Jerusalem when they heard a sound like a mighty rushing wind. It wasn't a wind, it was a sound. And when that sound ended, the thinking of those men and women was completely changed. Instead of hiding themselves in an upper room, they spilled out onto the streets boldly preaching about Jesus.

This whole idea about a transforming sound has been mulling around in my spirit for years and I have been studying everything I can find about sound, vibration, and frequency. I don't understand all that it means, but I feel like the Lord has told me if we will place our hearts in an upper room posture, He is again releasing a sound that will transform the way we think. I believe that sound is going to empower us to do greater works than He did.

The more I studied, the more I became convinced God is preparing to reveal kingdom insights about sound; and if we will receive and embrace these insights and revelations, we will finally become the children of God that creation has been eagerly awaiting.

Once I began the search to discover more about sound, God began leading me on a journey.

I read a book by Ted Dekker that mentioned quantum physics principles and the names of some leading quantum physicists. As I researched these men on the internet, I ran across an article by an astrophysicist named Bernard Haisch about the zero point field. Learning about the zero-point field made me want to study more about light, sound, energy, and vibrations.

The Zero-Point Field

Bernard Haisch's article is called *Brilliant Disguise: Light, Matter and the Zero-Point Field*[1] and in it he has this to say about the verse, "God said, 'Let there be light, and there was light.'"

> *It is certainly a beautiful poetic statement. But does it contain any science? A few years ago I would have dismissed that possibility. As an astrophysicist, I knew all too well the blatant contradictions between the sequence of events in Genesis and the physics of the Universe. Even after substituting eons for days, the order of events was obviously wrong. It made no sense to have light come first, and then to claim that the Sun, the moon and the stars—the obvious sources of light in the night sky of the ancient world—were created only subsequently, be it days or eons later. One could, of course, generalize light to mean simply energy, and thus claim a reference to the Big Bang, but that would, to me, be more of a stretch than a revelation.*

As soon as I read that paragraph, I looked up and saw God the Father at the beginning of time and I saw our universe with nothing in it. It was completely empty, formless and void. Then, the Father said, "Let there be light" and out of His being came wave after wave after wave of what appeared to be light. The light waves were curved, not straight. As I watched the light, I instantly thought, "Just like an artist prepares his canvas before he paints on it, God prepared our universe so he could create us, and the space in that universe needed light."

The Zero-Point Field

I immediately found a dictionary and looked up the definition of light. Two of the definitions were energy and power. I looked up the definition of energy: power and light. And the definition of power was energy and light. The meanings of the three words light, energy, and power are so interchangeable that they are used to define each other. This meant that in my vision the waves of light flowing from God's being could just as easily be called waves of energy or power because both are essentially the same thing as waves of light. In essence, I saw waves of all three—light, energy, and power.

Haisch's article continues:

Radio, television and cellular phones all operate by transmitting or receiving electromagnetic waves. Visible light is the same thing; it is just a higher frequency form of electromagnetic waves. At even higher frequencies, beyond the visible spectrum, you find ultraviolet light, X-rays and gamma-rays. All are electromagnetic waves which are really just different frequencies of light.

It is standard in quantum theory to apply the Heisenberg uncertainty principle to electromagnetic waves, since electric and magnetic fields flowing through space oscillate like a pendulum. At every possible frequency there will always be a tiny bit of electromagnetic jiggling going on. And if you add up all these ceaseless fluctuations, what you get is a background sea of light whose total energy is enormous: the zero-point field. The "zero-point" refers to the fact that even though this energy is huge, it is the lowest possible energy state. All other energy is over and above the zero-point state. Take any volume of space and take away everything else—in other words, create a vacuum—and what you are left with is the zero-point field. We can imagine a true vacuum, devoid of everything, but the real-world quantum vacuum is permeated by the zero-point field with its ceaseless electromagnetic waves.

The fact that the zero-point field is the lowest energy state makes it unobservable. We see things by way of contrast. The eye works by letting light fall on the otherwise dark retina. But if the eye were filled with light, there would be no darkness to afford a contrast.

The zero-point field is such a blinding light. Since it is everywhere, inside and outside of us, permeating every atom in our bodies, we are effectively blind to it. It blinds us to its presence. The world of light that we do see is all the rest of the light that is over and above the zero-point field.

But if we are right, then "Let there be light" is indeed a very profound statement, as one might expect of its purported author. The solid, stable world of matter appears to be sustained at every instant by an underlying sea of quantum light. In the reference frame of light, there is no space and time.

I was stunned. We live in a God-created universe sustained by an "underlying sea of quantum light" of immeasurable energy. One square yard of the zero-point field contains enough energy to boil all the water in the world. I believe that energy, that power, that light released by God at the beginning of time is what is in us and around us right now. That's God's power.

The Bible tells us, "'If you have the faith of a mustard seed, you can say to this mountain 'be removed' and it will be removed.'"

As I questioned God about whether we really have the power to move a mountain, I slowly realized that if this power within us is a zero-point field, if this power is what God first spoke into the creation of the earth because He wanted Adam and Eve to be powerful, then His original intent was for them to multiply and expand the Garden of Eden to the point where our entire world would be like an Eden. We'd all live together happily, and God would come and visit us. That was the Lord's original intent, yet because of sin it all changed. We became separated from God and were driven from the Garden.

The good news is that Jesus reconciled us back to God and to what we should have been in the garden of Eden, but our minds haven't been transformed enough yet to realize it.

I began to understand that if this world is actually going to be what it was created to be in the beginning, now that Jesus has redeemed everything we need to know what this power is, this "sea of quantum light" that undergirds everything. And, more importantly, we need to know how to access it.

We have the zero-point field within us. Individually, each of us may not have a square yard of zero-point field energy in us, but two or three of us together do, and the Bible says that whatever two or three agree on will be done. So we truly have the power within us and around us to move many, many mountains.

Jesus calmed storms. We should be able to do that too. Jesus healed the sick, cast out demons, raised the dead. We have that same power within us. And we also have power all around us, undergirding our universe.

Doing the "works" of Jesus and even "greater works" should be an everyday occurrence for us. When a child gets cancer, we should be able to tell that cancer to leave, now, because that child is not meant to die early; he is meant to have a long life. In the garden of Eden and up until the time of the flood people lived long lives. Psalm 90:10 says that we should live for 70 to 80 years and in Genesis 6: 3, God says man's "days should be an hundred and twenty years." This means everybody should be living until they are at least 70 because God has allotted each of us that amount of time on this earth.

But sometimes we don't even have to pray. Peter merely walked past people and every disease or infirmity his shadow passed over was healed. I imagine that he wasn't even aware people were being healed by his shadow until they told him. Peter carried the Spirit of God within him. He carried the original power of "let there be light"—energy, power, light—within him. And that's what we should be doing.

In this book, you will not only learn more about the mysteries of sound, light, vibrations, frequencies and energy, but you will also read the experiences of Bill Johnson, Beni

Johnson, Cal Pierce and others who were shaken by vibrations from God in such a way that they literally changed the way they thought.

Notes:

[1] If you want to know more about this subject, read Bernard Haish's book *The God Theory: Universes, Zero-Point Fields and What's Behind It All*, ©2009, Weiser Books.

 *Go to www.heavensphysics.com/chapter1 or scan this QR code on your smartphone to share your insights or spiritual experiences about topics covered in this chapter.*

Dolphins and Healing Energy

 For centuries there have been stories of spontaneous healings in the presence of dolphins but no scientific studies of this phenomenon until 1996, when the Upledger Foundation sponsored a project designed to investigate the effects of providing CranioSacral Therapy to patients while in the presence of dolphins. Patients involved in the dolphin-assisted treatments experienced a dramatic reduction in muscle restriction, a release of adhesions from past surgeries, a substantial reduction in pain, increased ease in breathing, enhanced strength and flexibility, increased appetite, and more restful sleep.

Since that time researchers have discovered that dolphins naturally produce an ultrasonic frequency that is four times the frequency used for therapeutic purposes in clinics and hospitals. Although no one really knows how dolphins heal, scientists speculate that dolphin ultrasound resonates with natural vibrational frequencies of the human body; that dolphins emit frequencies that synchronize right and left brain activity in humans; and that dolphins emit ultrasonic waves that positively alter human magnetic fields.

2

Extracting the Precious From the Worthless
by Ellyn Davis

In Jeremiah 15: 19, God says, "If you extract the precious from the worthless, you will become My spokesman." We may have to delve into areas we previously considered off-limits to extract the "precious" from the "worthless" and recover lost truths that belong to the people of God.

The Coming Golden Age

How did I develop an interest in energy, vibrations, and quantum physics? It all started in the 1960's when I was a hippie. That's right. I had the hair down to my waist, the bell-bottomed jeans, the tie-dyed T-shirts, the huarache sandals, and a passion to transform America's corrupt social systems and make the world a better place.

I had grown up in a staunch Baptist home, gone to church almost every time the doors opened and had at one time wanted to become a missionary. But as I entered my teen years, somehow the Christianity of my childhood seemed to have little relevance to my everyday life as a girl coming of age in the heart of the deep South during the tumultuous years of Civil Rights marches, Vietnam War protests, Feminist attempts to overthrow millennia of male domination, Timothy Leary's recommendations that we all "turn on, tune in, and drop out," and the race to be first to land on the moon. (And let's not forget Woodstock.).

Back then most of us had heard about the "New Age" that was coming—an age of love, peace, and enlightenment. Like in the song *Aquarius* from the Broadway hit *Hair*, it was to be an age of "harmony and understanding, sympathy and trust abounding, no more falsehoods or derisions…the mind's true liberation," a time when peace guided the planets and love steered the stars.

The times "they were a-changing" and we flower children wanted to do our part to accelerate the coming of this golden age.

What happened to me?

Well, the Golden Age never came about in the way we thought it might. Yes, the Civil Rights Act was finally passed, the Vietnam War eventually ground to a halt, women gradually were granted more equality with men than they had ever known, and Americans landed on the moon, not once, but six times.

However, for many of us, the beautiful dream of a New Age of love and peace went in one of two directions. The dream either became a nightmare as the flower children who wanted to "make love, not war" turned into homeless druggies and prostitutes or the dream just faded into the realities of responsibility as we former Hippies grew older, became Yuppies, and moved to the suburbs.

Extracting the Precious

I rejoined the "Establishment"; went to graduate school and got an M.S. in biochemistry; worked on my Ph.D. in virology; got married; had an encounter with the Holy Spirit that set me on fire for God; became a "Jesus Freak" for awhile; went into the ministry; had six children and several very successful businesses; and wrote three books. Meanwhile, all my youthful ideals and dreams of an era of love, peace and enlightenment were put on a back burner.

While my own dreams simmered, other former Hippies quietly morphed the dream of a new age into a multi-faceted belief system dedicated to achieving heightened spiritual consciousness.

This new consciousness was going to transform society not by protests or by "turning on, tuning in, and dropping out" but by developing powers of the mind, aligning with positive "energies," and removing physical, mental and emotional blockages to enlightenment. The burgeoning New Age movement began eagerly accepting and experimenting with Eastern and Native American religious practices, metaphysical philosophies, alternative healing methods, and altered states of consciousness.

Extracting the "precious" from the "worthless"

In 2006, through God's inexplicable sense of humor, I found myself with an empty nest and a job offer in Sedona, AZ, the global epicenter of New Age thought and practice. By then I had experienced most of what charismatic Christianity had to offer—miracles, prophecy, healing, deep revelation, transformative experiences of the presence of the Holy Spirit, excellent Bible teaching—and I had been involved in at least five modern-day moves of God in the church.

I moved to Sedona fully prepared to discount everything I saw and heard as coming from a source other than the God I knew and loved. But, as a scientist, I was intrigued by what I found there. I saw healings and mystical experiences and revelations to rival anything I had seen or experienced in the church. I encountered an understanding of the natural world and how it interacted with the spiritual that I had sensed but had never been taught in any of my science classes.

It wasn't that I wanted to become a New Ager, I just wanted to find out if maybe they had uncovered some truths the church hadn't. The strange thing was, much of what I saw and heard embodied biblical principles and could be backed up by Scripture.

When I was a little girl, I was so determined to discover the truth about everything that my father would tell his friends: "Ellyn's the kind of person who if you gave her a mountain of horse manure she'd spend all day shoveling through it saying, 'There's got to be a pony in here somewhere.'"

Well, I "shoveled a lot of manure" while I was in Sedona, and actually found some ponies. Of course, I found a lot of other things too—things that clearly could be attributed to too many drugs or the demonic realm or the fact that con-artists discovered they could make mega-bucks by becoming New Age gurus. But that didn't discourage me because I knew that mounds of "manure" usually go with the territory when a lot of money and prestige are at stake (remember, I had been in the ministry *and* in business for a long, long time).

Extracting the Precious

I was familiar with the principles that "whenever you see a counterfeit, it means a real exists" and that "a lie just proves the existence of a truth," so I decided to investigate what was going on and bring my scientific background and my faith in Jesus Christ into the mix of my search for truth. I decided to examine New Age thought and practice for anything "precious" that might be "extracted" from the worthless.

A lot of what I saw and heard in the New Age Movement embodied biblical principles and could be backed up by Scripture.

At that time, I could not find a single Christian leader who shared a similar interest in finding out if there were truths hidden in the New Age. Now we are beginning to hear more and more revelation that is in line with what New Agers have been saying all along and we are hearing more and more teaching about Christians "taking back truths" from the New Age that really belong to citizens of the Kingdom of God.

The Time Delay

It usually takes 50 years or longer for scientific theory to become embedded in mainstream thought. For example, Einstein published his general theory of relativity in 1916, but it wasn't until the 1960's that the philosophy of "relativism" became part of the thinking of the general public. Phrases like "it's all relative" or "truth is what's true for you" crept into mainstream vocabulary and by the 1980's courses about situational ethics were being taught in classrooms and corporate boardrooms across the nation.

So a 1916 scientific theory about how time and the speed of light are not absolute but relative to the frame of reference was transmuted by philosophers and social scientists into the 1980's concept that truth, morality, and ethics are always relative to some particular frame of reference, such as a time period or a culture.

The scientific theories currently filtering into mainstream thinking mainly have to do with mystical interpretations of quantum physics.

We live in a decade when 21 million copies of the book *The Secret* have been sold, when over half a million people tuned in to Oprah Winfrey's 10 week online seminar with Eckhart Tolle discussing his book *The New Earth* and when there are over three and a half million New Agers worldwide who embrace some sort of philosophical/spiritual spin on the quantum physics theories of the early to mid-twentieth century.

Just what is "quantum mysticism?" According to Wikipedia, "Quantum mysticism is a term that has been used to refer to a set of metaphysical beliefs and associated practices that seek to relate consciousness, intelligence or mystical world-views to the ideas of quantum mechanics and its interpretations."

Many in the church have tended to write off all dabblings into quantum mysticism as blasphemous and demonically inspired. However, there are a few courageous Christians who are beginning to speak up and say, "Wait a minute, there may be some God truth there that really belongs to us and that we should know about!"

These Christians are spearheading an effort to extract the precious from the worthless and make those truths available to the church at large.

We are hearing more and more teachings about Christians "taking back truths" from the New Age that really belong to the Kingdom of God

---

Skating to the Puck

Jonathan Edwards, the legendary 18th century minister once said, "A work of God without stumbling blocks is never to be expected." I believe that a great work of God is in process as He restores knowledge and insights that have been lost to Christians but are now hidden in the teachings and practices of Quantum Mysticism.

There are many stumbling blocks to be expected as we extract "precious" truths from the "worthless," but I refuse to let one of those stumbling blocks be my fear that I will somehow be tainted or captured by the devil as I try to recover and express those truths.

Hockey great Wayne Gretzky once shared the secret to his success. He said, "I skate to where the puck is going to be, not where it has been." As Christians, we tend to keep "skating where the puck has been" instead of where it's going to be. In other words, we get comfortable with what God has done and we tend to camp there, even when He's moved on or is giving us new revelation. Why? Because almost every time God "moves on" He takes us into unfamiliar territory that seems dangerous and sometimes seems to contradict what He's done in the past.

The greatest examples of God seeming to contradict Himself and the Church being slow to accept that the "puck" had been moved are found in Acts—first when Peter was told in a vision to eat unclean animals and secondly when Paul announced that the promises of God are for Gentiles as well as Jews. Both "moves of the puck" were met with astonishment and disbelief.

Towards the end of his life, I was fortunate to sit under the teaching of Ern Baxter. In his younger years, Ern had been an associate of William Branham, so he had seen more healings and miracles than almost anyone I have ever met. When I met Ern, he had lived through multiple moves of God and had this to say about them, "When the Holy Spirit moves on, all that's left is dove dung."

I believe that the Holy Spirit is moving again. So do all of the Christian leaders who contributed to this book. They are all trying to position themselves to be "where the puck is going to be," not where it's been.

None of them want to be caught in the "dove dung" left behind when the Spirit moves on. They all agree that the next move of God will cause a shift at the deepest level of who we are—perhaps at the very "vibrational level" that the New Age movement has been exploring. They also all agree that there are precious truths hidden in the New Age that belong to us as Christians and need to be extracted from the worthless.

Extracting the Precious

New Paradigms of Reality

If you study the history of science, you will realize that less than 250 years ago people believed diseases were caused by "vapors." Only heretics suspected that tiny, unseen organisms might exist until Louis Pasteur confirmed the germ theory of disease, a theory that has become the mainstay of modern medicine.

Today the old paradigm we are having a hard time releasing is the paradigm of reality being what we can see, hear, smell, touch, manipulate, and measure with instrumentation. Observations, insights, and practices that don't fit into that paradigm of reality are considered mystical or "paranormal." But remember, it's just been in the last century that we have developed quantum physics and the atom bomb as well as discovered the earth's vibrational frequency, brainwaves, and the electromagnetic field of the human heart. We can't be so arrogant as to think that today's paradigm of reality won't one day be as outmoded as the "vapors" theory of disease.

This book just touches the tip of the iceberg of what is being discovered about sound, light, energy, frequencies, and vibrations. There are mysteries of God and nature we are only beginning to delve into. My hope is that this voyage of discovery we are taking together allows you to be open to deeper understandings of God's reality.

Go to www.heavensphysics.com/chapter2 or scan this QR code on your smartphone to share your insights and spiritual experiences about topics covered in this chapter.

Squeamish Yet?

At this point, you are probably asking yourself, "What do dolphins and energy and vibrations and frequencies and quantum physics and zero-point theory have to do with the Kingdom of God?"

These are all good questions that we hope to answer in the rest of this book. But remember, we warned you in the beginning that we don't really know all the answers yet. We're on a voyage of discovery into realms that may contain mysteries of God, but, then again, they may not. And because we've never been this way before, we're not exactly sure how to navigate this journey and don't know what dragons we may face.

If you've read this far in the book, you know our (Judy's and Ellyn's) stories of how we became interested in such weird and wonderful phenomena as energy, frequencies, vibrations, and quantum physics. You should also be aware that we suspect God is up to something new—something that will transform us at the deepest level of who we are and will be ushered in by a new form of "sound" or "vibration."

Let's just take this journey together and see what we might discover....

3

Vibrating in Harmony With God
by Bob Jones

In this chapter, written from interviews, Bob Jones shares that God is beginning to "breathe" on His people again to prepare us for a second Pentecost that "tunes" us and brings us into harmony with God.

God recently showed me that shields were being given to different men and women. You know what a shield is, like a badge? You put it over your heart, and the Holy Spirit is giving shields to people to represent authority here on earth. The shields I saw were both for men and women in authority.

What is the power in a badge or shield? Let's say in Redding there's a guy who's been training to be a policeman. He finishes his training and he's given a shield. But when he goes out on the streets and directs traffic, people begin to heckle him and stop the traffic. They are trying to overpower his authority. This policeman can put out a call to every person who has a shield in Redding and all the other policeman in Redding will come to his defense. If that doesn't work, the police department can call the governor who can call in the national guard. If the national guard can't resolve the problem, they can call the president, and the president can put all the "shield people" on alert to come to the aid of that one policeman. That's the authority of a person who has a shield.

So, shields have been given to both men and women because these men and women have gone through various testings to receive them. They have been given a badge to go right over their heart. And that badge has authority in it. I don't think there are that many people God's going to give shields to yet, but the people who have shields will begin to bring a divine order.

That badge is like a blank check and it has the number 341 on it. Both men and women are being given the authority of badges and there are six things they have "blank checks" to do: healing, holy confiscation, prayer, petitioning, teaching, and ushering in prosperity. Prosperity will go from one group to another. Those who are prepared will have it all there when others need it.

We are being prepared for the Second Pentecost

When the first Pentecost came, there were tongues of fire and they received other languages. There was a mighty rushing wind, or breath, or I would call it a portal right into heaven and the men and women at Pentecost were underneath that portal. They were commissioned that day, they got their badges. One hundred and twenty of them had been faithful and had gone through the training.

Those 50 days beforehand were the training. They were faithful, they graduated. They were given their badges of authority, their shields. And that's what they began to do. To shield our church and birth into our church. They turned the world right side up because it was in a mess. Their words were heard in all languages. In other words, their tongues spoke all languages, and the people from all nations heard it. I believe there's coming a time when all nations will hear. And again, I don't believe we've received the fullness of Pentecost.

When God breathes on a thing, it smells like apples. It says in Song of Solomon 7:8, "and his breath smells like apples." I've smelled apples in meetings several different times.

So I believe God is getting ready to breathe on us—the "ruach." And we need to know what His breath smells like. Stop everything and let that breath come on you.

The 120 at Pentecost spoke in other tongues. They were instantly able to speak other languages. There are people today who have received 5 or 6 languages instantaneously, but that hasn't really happened to many of us yet. That's what I believe is waiting for us—when the fullness of Pentecost comes we will be able to converse with people in every language and understand them. It happened with the 120, didn't it? Everyone listening heard the disciples speak the native tongue of their own land, from different countries all over the world.

You've asked me, "What do you think the sound was that came?" and you've mentioned a vibration. I believe the vibration takes place in us. There are negative and positive vibrations. A positive vibration is like a portal into heaven. A negative vibration is like cancer. When the power comes, the positive will kill the negative. It's a vibration. Everything vibrates... rocks, trees, everything vibrates.

When we vibrate I think it's opening a portal. The Old Testament speaks of windows or doors into heaven and there are 300 of them. To me they're like a funnel or a portal. There are 28 of them in the New Testament. Revelations 4:1 is about an open heaven, but it's really about an open portal and heaven coming down and touching earth. This is what I think happened on the day of Pentecost.

I believe God is getting ready to breathe on us—the "ruach." And we need to know what His breath smells like. Stop everything and let that breath come on you.

What was given on the day of Pentecost? The Holy Spirit. Jesus did everything He did as a man, as a God/man, in obedience. But when He ascended on high the Holy Spirit was given to Him and He released it on the day of Pentecost. What we're talking about in the fullness of Pentecost is a release of the Holy Spirit beyond imagination and description.

I've studied a lot of scripture about when the fullness of Pentecost comes. When it says in Hebrews 6:1, "And having tasted the good word of God," that was the power of Pentecost. But when it says, "and then the power of the world to come," that's millennial power. The power of the world to come will be 10 times that of Pentecost. It's like the difference between the tabernacle of Moses and the temple of

Solomon. The temple of Solomon was 10 times greater than the tabernacle. We're talking about 10 times the power that was released at Pentecost. And the glory of the latter house will be 10 times greater than of the former.

So I believe we've been prepared for the fullness of Pentecost and I've really been praying "Lord, is it this year?" I know we're getting close to it. We haven't received Pentecost yet. We received a token 110 years ago. But we didn't get the main. We're being prepared for the main Pentecost and millennial power, our priesthood power. We're being prepared for the priesthood of Melchizedek, and not only to be holy priests but also kings—living stones united together, vibrating together.

There's a new sound coming

We began having prophecies in 1995 that there is a new sound coming, a new heavenly sound. It's going to come in everything and it's especially going to come in praise. A couple of times recently, only for a little bit, I've been in beautiful praise when all of a sudden a new sound comes that I've never heard before. It's like it sets you on fire. The new sound is a string instrument, a wind instrument. So there's a new sound coming.

One time, years ago in Atlanta I was at a church with Rick Joyner and there was a sound that seemed to be coming out of the ceiling. Everybody heard it. It had an angel power with it.

This coming new sound isn't just something that you pick up with your ears, but it's greater than anything you can understand. It can change DNA so we are genetically growing up. Your genetics are the same as His was. Our genetics come out of the Father in our spirit. We are becoming like an instrument being tuned, where our genetics are getting aligned with the Father's genetics, in harmony with Him.

Do you know what a heart fibrillation is? It's two hearts. The lower heart gets out of harmony with the upper heart. And I'm afraid that our spiritually lower heart has gotten out of harmony with our upper heart, but when it gets back in harmony we'll have the heart of God.

> *This coming new sound isn't just something that you pick up with your ears, but it's greater than anything you can understand, It can change DNA so we are genetically growing up. We are becoming like an instrument being tuned, where our genetics are getting aligned with the Father's genetics, in harmony with Him.*

The recent earthquakes and tsunamis are a natural shifting in the earth and a change in the axis of the earth and change in even nations. It's only natural that there is a spiritual changing of nations too. These changes are occurring for what purpose? We've turned away from God. These shiftings are to turn us back to God.

With all these earthquakes and the shifting of the earth's axis, it's almost like the whole world has been out of align-

Vibrating in Harmony with God

ment and everything is being "tuned." But it's about tuning everything, not just the earth. It's about tuning us and everything about us. When we get in harmony with God and begin to really worship the Father in spirit and truth, there's no time there. You'll think that you've been in it a minute and I've known times when we were in worship for hours, and it only felt like minutes. We're going to take authority over everything down here back and literally give it back to the Father.

With me, when I had a fibrillation, they took me to the hospital and gave me an electrical shock. The shock brought my upper and lower heart back into harmony. There are shocks down here that are going to bring us back into harmony with our Father. That "vibration" put my heart back into harmony. They called it "conversion." So I think a good word for what's about to happen to us is "a conversion."

Isaiah 66:2 says, "I will look to him who trembles at my word." The word "trembles" in this verse can be vibration. And everything vibrates. But when we get in harmony with God, everything will vibrate in tune with us. Total authority was given to man. Do you have any idea what everything vibrating in harmony with God would do in the earth?

This chapter was excerpted from interviews with Bob Jones.

Go to www.heavensphysics.com/chapter3 or scan this QR code on your smartphone to share your insights and spiritual experiences about topics covered in this chapter.

Healing Energy

From the point of view of quantum physics, as human beings we are not only immersed in energy fields, but our bodies, and our minds *are* energy fields. Researchers are now studying ways to work with the body's energy to bring healing. Dr. Mehmet Oz, of TV fame, reflected the opinion of many medical professionals when he recently stated, "As we get a better understanding of how little we know about the body, we begin to realize that the next big frontier in medicine is energy medicine."

There are many well established uses of energy fields in the diagnosis and treatment of disease. Some of these include: magnetic resonance imaging, laser eye correction surgery, cardiac pacemakers, radiation therapy, and UV light therapies for psoriasis and seasonal affective disorder. There are also a few less-researched therapies that use energy fields such as music therapy, using magnets to increase blood flow, and the use of tuning forks to produce healing sound frequencies.

However, there is growing interest in the unmeasurable energy fields in diagnosis and treatment of disease.

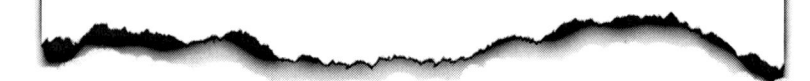

4

Recovering Our Spiritual Inheritance
by Bill Johnson

While this chapter isn't about sound, vibrations, or frequencies, we wanted to put Bill Johnson's teaching on recovering our spiritual inheritance in this book because there are whole realms of insights that belong to the people of God we've failed to explore and, therefore, haven't been leaving as a legacy for future generations. Read on, as Bill Johnson explains when the Church stops "taking things forward," a vacuum forms that the enemy fills. He emphasizes how crucial it is for us to recover lost "God truths" as an inheritance to future generations of Christians.

We often speak of laying up a spiritual inheritance for future generations, but what exactly do we mean? What is an inheritance?

An inheritance in the natural can be anything a person values enough to leave to the next generation. It usually is either property or money and represents years and years of another person's effort. If you receive an inheritance when you're younger, say as a young, newly married adult, that inheritance can financially "jump start" your ability to have things that otherwise would have taken you years to obtain.

You might be able to buy a house, or live in a part of town only people higher up the corporate ladder can afford. You might be able to pay for your college education or buy a nice car. An inheritance allows you to start out ahead of where you would have been without it. With an inheritance, you receive for free what others worked to have.

A spiritual inheritance works the same way. It enables us to start our Christian life at spiritual levels that might normally have taken us years to reach. Another generation's "ceiling" in God can become our spiritual "floor."

However this is seldom what happens. The tragic record of history is that no revival has ever made it a priority to leave a spiritual inheritance to the next generation. That means each new revival started from scratch and only built for its generation, so we've only seen what one generation can accomplish in God. We've never seen the accelerated spiritual growth that comes from inheritance. We've never fully seen what a spiritual "jump start" can mean to the next generation.

Moves of God come and go, and usually by the second or third generation the precious truths that the first generation embraced and fought so strongly to maintain have been either distorted or forgotten. Those who began in the move of God had no plan to pass on what they discovered to the ones who would follow them. So much of their revelation of God's power, His presence, and His ways died with them.

Unclaimed Mantles

There are anointings, mantles, revelations and mysteries that have lain unclaimed, literally where they were left, because the generation that walked in them never passed them on. I believe it's possible for us to recover realms of anointing, realms of insight, realms of God that have been untended for decades simply by choosing to reclaim them and perpetuate them for future generations.

Proverbs says that a righteous man leaves an inheritance to his children's children. That means righteousness, when it has a true effect on your heart, forces you to see that your decisions today have a domino effect on multiple generations following you. My decision today will affect generations beyond me. How do I want to affect them?

Deuteronomy 29:29 says, "The secret things belong to the Lord our God, but those things which are revealed belong to us and to our children forever, that we may do all the words of this law." This passage is amazing. It says, "the secret things belong to the Lord," yet in the New Testament Jesus says, "It's the Father's good pleasure to give you the secrets of the Kingdom."

Jesus taught in parables, not to reveal truth, but to hide truth. Truth is not hidden from you; it's hidden *for* you. "It's the glory of God to conceal a matter; it's the glory of kings to search it out." God is glorified by not speaking in plain language to you. He's glorified by speaking in parables, symbols and dark sayings. The royalty that exists in the life of the believer—we've been called a "royal priesthood"—comes to the surface when we realize we have legal access to hidden things and we begin to pursue the unlocking of those mysteries. God has given access to the secret realms of science, of politics, of business, of creativity in the arts, for example.

There are realms opening up right now to people because they realize their destiny. They realize that God has ordained and given them access to hidden things.

Jesus said, "The things that are revealed are for you and your children forever." That means that once a truth has been revealed to the people of God, it is never to be forgotten.

I believe it's possible for us to recover realms of anointing, realms of insight, realms of God that have been untended for decades simply by choosing to reclaim them and perpetuate them for future generations.

The Purpose of Revelation

Revelation does not come to us to make us smarter. Revelation does not come so that we can have a more complete doctrinal statement. Revelation comes for three basic reasons. First, to bring us personal transformation Second, to move truth forward, and third, to create a legacy of inheritance for future generations.

When revelation comes to us, it is intended to launch us into a divine encounter that allows us to advance the kingdom of God.

A divine encounter is what rearranges our perspective in life. Divine encounters keep knowledge from being so dangerous. The Bible says, "Knowledge puffs up." Knowledge in and of itself will make everyone arrogant. Knowledge puffs up because it just equips us to debate with other Christians. But when revelation knowledge has a divine encounter, we're in less danger of pride.

When Paul was knocked off his donkey in his encounter with God, he didn't strut away from the encounter boasting, "Wait till you see the books I'm about to write! I'm going to change the course of church history." You don't see that arrogance in him because the revelation, as grand as it was, was equaled by divine encounter. Revelation knowledge that doesn't take us into a divine encounter only makes us more religious. Jesus said in John 5:39-40, "You search the Scriptures, for in them you think you have eternal life; and these are they which testify of Me. But you are not willing to come to Me that you may have life." The Scripture is to launch you into an encounter with Christ.

So the first reason for revelation is personal transformation. The second reason is that revelation enlarges the playing field of our faith. If you think that Jesus makes people sick because He has a divine purpose to work in them, then you've got a very small playing field for your faith to work in. But when you see that Jesus heals because of righteousness—it's the Sun of Righteousness who rises with healing in His wings (Malachi 4:2)—you have a wider field of faith.

It's out of His righteousness that Jesus vindicates the effect of sin in the world by healing disease and delivering from affliction. You also see that Jesus healed every person who came to Him and turned no one away and that He is the exact representation of the Father.

Recovering Spiritual Inheritance

Everything else previous to this was type and shadow, which means that you need to challenge any knowledge you have about God that you can't find in the person of Jesus.

I want to make sure you get this message out of Deuteronomy because it sets a stunning precedent throughout Scripture. When truth is given to the Church, truth is always to lead to divine encounter, never to be departed from but only built upon.

Revelation comes for three basic reasons. First, to bring us personal transformation. Second, to move truth forward, and third, to create a legacy of inheritance for future generations.

Truth Should Always Move Forward

When truth came to the early Church, it was to increase and be passed to the next generation. It was only meant to go in forward motion, yet that didn't happen. But we have an opportunity in this generation to grab the concept of spiritual inheritance and see, for the first time in church history, what it looks like. We have the opportunity to lay ourselves down for a generation we'll never see, so they can build on our ceiling and take it to places in God we never had time to go.

Let's look at Luke 11:24-26:

When an unclean spirit goes out of a man, he goes through dry places, seeking rest; and finding none, he says, "I will return to my house from which I came." And when he comes, he finds it swept and put in order. Then he goes and takes with him seven other spirits more wicked than himself, and they enter and dwell there; and the last state of that man is worse than the first.

This sounds like a strange passage to throw in with the concept of spiritual inheritance. But there is a principle of the Kingdom in this passage that is vital for us to understand and that principle is this: We have the opportunity to recover lost wealth of prior generations that was, for whatever reason, disregarded.

I have no finger to point or bone to pick. But there were realms of God that were entered into in past generations that were neglected. Who knows the reasons? I don't even care. All I know is that there are realms of God, realms of past triumphs and victories that the Church entered into that are not a present day experience. It's a tragedy because He said, "The things that are revealed are yours and your children's forever."

Luke 11:24-26 is a picture of a house. A house in Scripture can refer to an individual. In this case it's talking about a person who goes through deliverance. A house can refer to a physical house—a house of God where people worship. It also can refer to occupation. There are a number of things that it points to throughout Scripture. Let me illustrate it this way. If the measure of triumph and victory that a person comes into is not maintained, it becomes re-occupied by the enemy.

Israel, in the Old Testament, was given the Promised Land, and the Lord said, "I've got good news and I've got bad news.

The good news is that it's all yours. The bad news is that you get it little by little." As they grew in maturity and had the capability of stewarding what was released to them, God would release more land. If He gave it to them all at once, He said it would be too big for them. They wouldn't be able to occupy it, and because they wouldn't be able to occupy it, it would be filled with beasts that would multiply and destroy the people. It's a strange thing, but the Lord allows the enemy to occupy some things to preserve them for us.

So the Lord releases areas of territory. But the tragedy is when the baton is passed to the next generation, they fail to occupy and advance the territory given. Did you know that the only safe place for a believer is in the realm of advancement?

Occupation by itself will destroy you. It's not a safe place. Ask the guy who buried one talent to protect what he had. God's Kingdom is so focused on increase and advancement that the most dangerous place to be is to have and protect something and not consider it useful for advancement.

Advancement Is The Nature of the Kingdom

Advancement is the nature of the Kingdom. It's always increasing. Regardless of circumstances that surround you, never interpret the purpose and plan of the Lord on the earth according to your restricted, small, personal experience. We must think in terms of a bigger picture, where God's Kingdom is constantly advancing.

We are all soldiers in an army laying down our lives so that the kingdoms of this world would become the kingdoms of our Lord and of His Christ (Revelations 11:15).

Let's put this in perspective. What if your bank called you up and said, "A distant cousin just died and left you ten million dollars. It has already been deposited into your bank account." Do you think you'd spend money a little differently tomorrow than you did yesterday? Some of you would jump up right away and head for the mall. Others would begin looking for a financial adviser.

Spiritually, you have an even greater inheritance than ten million dollars. Our responsibility as biblical teachers is to teach you how to spend your spiritual inheritance wisely.

Where Do We Start?

We can begin by recovering secrets, mysteries, mantles, and realms of God that have been abandoned and ignored for decades, some of them for centuries. They just lie there waiting for someone in this generation to come along and claim them. What do you think the Lord has been doing in recent days, when He stirs people to write books about "re-digging the wells"? God is saying, "There are things that are lying there, mysteries to be understood, inheritances that are untended, uncared for, unoccupied. But they're there for the taking."

At the same time we need to start thinking and planning and sowing into a generation we will never see. It's time to start constructing in our thinking, in our planning and our prayers, a hundred-year vision.

We have a history of two thousand years of unusual things. None of them were meant to be lost, but all maintained, and all built upon and expanded. Though I don't have a clear enough perspective on history, I have this sense that because of this place where we are in the unfolding of history, we may be in a position that no other generation has ever been. We may be the generation who actually carries things forward in God.

God is saying, "There are mysteries to be understood, inheritances that are untended, uncared for, unoccupied. But they're there for the taking."

Do you know why we're surrounded by a cloud of witnesses? In a relay race you can have the fastest runner on the planet run the first leg of the race. He can pass the baton to the second fastest runner on the planet, who can pass the baton to the third fastest runner on the planet. But everyone gets a prize according to how the last leg of the race is run. They're all waiting to see what we will do with what we've been given.

We've been given an inheritance of generations. We've been given an inheritance of hundreds of years of mystics, of revivalists, of those who broke into realms of the Spirit to leave something as an inheritance, and it needs to matter to someone.

Discovering the "secret things" that God has left for us has to matter. I believe one of the keys is for us to come to the place where we recover lost mysteries of God by learning how to give honor to those who are willing to sacrifice to make sure those mysteries are reclaimed.

There has never been a generation who has fully lived out of an inheritance. Yet inheritance is the nature of God;

it's the nature of Scripture; it's the nature of the moves of God. It was supposed to be that way from the beginning.

*This chapter is adapted with permission from Bill Johnson's audio series **Spiritual Inheritance**.*

Go to www.heavensphysics.com/chapter4 or scan this QR code on your smartphone to share your insights and spiritual experiences about topics covered in this chapter.

Healing Energy

The small Kirlian photo on the left shows electrical energy radiating from the hand of a healer. Scientists have just recently begun to study and measure the energy of healing and their findings are astonishing.

Electrical and Magnetic Measurements. Healing practitioners can emit powerful pulsing biomagnetic fields from their hands in the same frequency range that biomedical researchers use to help accelerate healing of soft and hard tissue injuries. These fields are about 1000 times stronger than the strongest human biomagnetic fields.

Brain wave activity in healers. Studies of brain wave activity in "healers" from all over the world (psychics, shamans, Christian faith healers, Hawaiian kahunas, etc.) have shown that during healing moments the healers' brain waves became phase and frequency synchronized with the earth's geoelectric micropulsations—the Schumann resonance.

Temperature: During energy healing, the temperature of the healer's hand rises as much as 4 degrees.

Infrasonic Sound. Researchers in China report exceptionally high-intensity infrasonic emissions from the hands of more seasoned healers.

5

Authentic vs. Counterfeit
by Jonathan Welton

"...But as his anointing teaches you about all things...that anointing is real, not counterfeit..." (1 John 2:27). Jonathan Welton teaches that whenever there is a real, there is sure to be a counterfeit. We shouldn't be afraid to examine the counterfeits because God's power to keep us is mightier than the devil's power to steal us away. Jonathan tells us that we need to be much more concerned about reclaiming all of our stolen goods from the enemy than about being afraid of the deception of counterfeits.

A thought came to me as I walked the aisles of my local Christian bookstore. I kept noticing row after row of what I call "response" books. A response book is a book written in reaction to the secular entertainment world. Typically these are written regarding the mega best sellers of the day or the blockbuster hit movies and most especially in reference to the flavor of the month fads: a series about romantic vampires, a young British witch, or a movie about the lost Gnostic gospels. Once the secular world produces a success, Christian authors take to the task of writing a slew of reactionary books.

Authentic vs. Counterfeit

This approach puts the church on the defensive in engaging the world. Our time is not best served by pointing out the darkness that surrounds us; we are to display our light. Considering that two of the best fiction writers of the 20th century, C.S. Lewis and J.R.R. Tolkien, were devout Christians, the church has the power to shine brightly in the darkness.

We cannot spend precious time on the defensive against the onslaught of evil in the secular entertainment world. I would like to present a new strategy. Each time we see the kingdom of darkness highlighted through books, movies, etc., we should ask, "What is this a counterfeit of in the Kingdom of Light?"

Throughout the Bible we see that everything Satan does is a mere counterfeit of something from God's Kingdom. Apostle Paul calls these counterfeits, "masquerades."

If the nature of the devil were to be studied throughout the Bible, we would find that the only thing he can do is take something that God has created and distort it into something different and worse than it was originally meant to be.

Counterfeits Reveal Authenticity

This brings us to the most important point of this chapter. If there is a counterfeit, there is an authentic that we need to find and reclaim. Every time we see a masquerade, we need to look closely to properly discern what is being counterfeited, because a counterfeit is evidence that an authentic exists.

Consider the example of counterfeit money. If there is counterfeit money, it proves that there is real, authentic money. Just because counterfeit money exists, we do not burn all our real money to avoid deception. The best response would be to get as many people as possible to use real money, so that when counterfeit money appears, it is recognizable by all. The fact that there are people operating in counterfeit miracles proves that there are real miracles available to the Church.

As Christians, when we see that Satan has created a counterfeit, we commonly overreact to try to protect ourselves from contamination. One way that we overreact is by throwing out anything that looks like the counterfeit, including the real. This is like burning all the money in your wallet because there are counterfeits in the world and deception is possible.

Each time we see the kingdom of darkness highlighted through books, movies, etc., we should ask, "What is this a counterfeit of in the Kingdom of Light?"

We have been commissioned not to throw out all things, but to "Test everything. Hold on to the good" (1 Thess. 5:21). Therefore, if we see a counterfeit, we must test it and find out what it counterfeits so we can reclaim the authentic.

Consider taking this as a personal challenge: If you see a counterfeit, use it as a signpost that points to the authentic.

The Source

To test all counterfeits, both natural and spiritual, you must determine the source. A real Rembrandt painting is authentic because Rembrandt painted it. With counterfeit currency the question is, "Did this bill originate from the official government mint?" It does not matter that the counterfeit money or paintings look similar to the originals: the best counterfeit looks as close to the original as possible, and it is difficult to tell the difference. The test of authenticity is always about origin. This is true of money, paintings, and the spirit realm.

Many Christians have been afraid to reclaim the authentic because they consider the power of the counterfeit to be overwhelmingly deceiving. The perception is that one could accidentally fall over the edge and suddenly be operating in the counterfeit without meaning to.

Personally, I have a lot more faith in the Lord's ability to keep me than in the devil's ability to steal me away. Jesus said that He has us in His hand and no one can snatch us out. "I give them eternal life, and they shall never perish; no one can snatch them out of My hand" (John 10:28).

If we are asking the Lord to restore the authentic to us, why should we have so much fear of accidentally operating in the counterfeit? Jesus said:

Which of you fathers, if your son asks for a fish, will give him a snake instead? Or if he asks for an egg, will give him a scorpion? If you then, though you are evil, know how to give good gifts to your children, how much more will your Father in heaven give the Holy Spirit to those who ask Him! (Luke 11:11-13)

There is no need to fear the supernatural if you are a Christian. God has you in His hand. If we are asking for the

Authentic vs. Counterfeit

Holy Spirit to do something, we do not need to fear receiving a counterfeit. The way that God moves in power looks a lot like the New Age, and this has scared many Christians away from operating in the gifts of the Holy Spirit.

The truth is that the gifts of the Holy Spirit will look similar to the counterfeit. The best counterfeits resemble what they are made to imitate. Because the counterfeit and the authentic will always look incredibly similar; the main test is the origin.

If there is a counterfeit, there is an authentic that we need to find and reclaim. Every time we see a masquerade, we need to look closely to properly discern what is being counterfeited, because a counterfeit is evidence that an authentic exists. The fact that there are people operating in counterfeit miracles proves that there are real miracles available to the Church.

We need to be much more concerned about reclaiming all of our stolen goods from the enemy than about being afraid of the deception of counterfeits.

The Test

One reason it has become increasingly difficult to discern the counterfeit from the authentic is that the New Age movement has been adopting Christian language for the past several decades. They honor Jesus as a good prophet, claim to interact with the "white light" of the Holy Spirit, and they speak of God as their Father. This can confuse a Christian who does not recognize the subtle but important differences between their language and the truth of God's Word. I have stated that the main difference between a counterfeit and the authentic is its source, but we need to be even more specific about how to discern between the two.

The test of what power source a person is operating in can be boiled down to the question, "Is Jesus the Lord of their life?" According to Romans 10:9-10, a person must acknowledge that Jesus was raised from the dead and that Jesus is the Lord of his or her life. If a person will not agree with these two things, then it is a fact that they are operating from a source other than the true Jesus of the Bible.

Spiritual practitioners who access and operate in the spirit without Jesus as the Lord of their lives are trespassers in the spirit realm. Jesus put it this way. "I tell you the truth, the man who does not enter the sheep pen by the gate, but climbs in by some other way, is a thief and a robber" (John 10:1).

Spiritual practitioners who access and operate in the spirit without Jesus as the Lord of their lives are trespassers in the spirit realm.

So to answer the common question, "Are psychics and New Agers operating in real power?" The answer is yes, but they have climbed in as trespassers. They have not accessed the spirit realm through Jesus.

Authentic vs. Counterfeit

Without receiving the death, resurrection, and forgiveness of Jesus, we are not in right relationship with the Father. Without right relationship, we are trespassing when we enter into spiritual experiences, and we can be easily deceived and destroyed. It is dangerous to operate in spiritual realms without being in right relationship with the Lord of heaven and earth. We must go into the sheepfold through the gate, which is Jesus Christ.

There are many people who claim Jesus in their spiritual practices but they have not actually submitted themselves to His lordship. I believe that these are the people Jesus was speaking of when He said:

> *Not everyone who says to Me, "Lord, Lord," will enter the kingdom of heaven, but only he who does the will of my Father who is in heaven. Many will say to Me on that day, "Lord, Lord, did we not prophesy in Your name, and in Your name drive out demons and perform many miracles?" Then I will tell them plainly, "I never knew you. Away from me, you evildoers!" (Matthew 7:21-23)*

Unfortunately, many Christians have beat themselves up wondering if they are those to whom Jesus was referring in this passage. The truth is that this group is comprised of people who use Jesus' name but have no personal, experiential, relationship with Him.

Resistance

As we have seen so far, there are many people who operate in the supernatural. Some operate safely under the lordship of

Authentic vs. Counterfeit

Jesus Christ and some, such as Buddhists, Hindus, New Agers, and Occultists, operate dangerously as trespassers.

For the normal Christian reclaiming the supernatural, the greatest resistance actually does not come from those who are walking in the counterfeit but rather from a third group. Here are the three perspectives regarding the operation of the supernatural as I see it.

1. Those walking in the authentic.
2. Those walking in the counterfeit.
3. Those walking in neither who are afraid of groups 1 and 2.

Interestingly, group 1 (Christians operating in the power of the Holy Spirit) typically receive the most opposition not from group 2 (false religionists operating out of evil power sources) but actually from group 3 (fellow Christians who believe false doctrines regarding the operation of supernatural power).

The counterfeit and the authentic look so similar that group 3 frequently declares that group 1 is walking in the counterfeit. This what the Pharisees said of Jesus.

One day Jesus cast out a demon from a mute man, and when the demon was gone, the man began to speak. The crowds were amazed, but some of them said, "No wonder he can cast out demons. He gets his power from Satan, the prince of demons" (Luke 11:14-15).

Like the Pharisees, the modern religious spirit does not understand that the existence of the false proves that there is an authentic. Instead of asking God for discernment to tell the difference, the Pharisees determined that if they look the same, then they are the same.

Authentic vs. Counterfeit

Considering that even Jesus Himself was accused of walking in dark, supernatural power, we should be prepared for the same accusation. As we reclaim our God-given gifts, there will always be those who accuse us of falling prey to the counterfeit.

Being a normal Christian is not for the faint of heart. There will always be those who resist the Holy Spirit. But what may surprise you (as you become normal) is that the strongest resistance does not come from the sinner but from the fellow saint.

Like the Pharisees, the modern religious spirit does not understand that the existence of the false proves that there is an authentic.

Counterfeits to Reclaim

With all this talk about counterfeit and authentic, by now you may be scratching your head hoping for examples. The best examples I have found are in the New Age Movement. They have been trafficking in the church's stolen goods for a long time.

I have found throughout Scripture at least 75 examples of things that the New Age has counterfeited, such as having a spirit guide, trances, meditation, auras, power objects, clairvoyance, clairaudience, and more. These actually belong to the church, but they have been stolen and cleverly repackaged. These examples have been included to stretch you and get you thinking differently about some of the ways that we have reacted when we see the counterfeits. Now whenever you see a counterfeit, I hope you will ask yourself these questions, "What is that a counterfeit of? What is its source? How can I have the authentic?"

The Commission

Imagine that the Church had a warehouse full of 10,000 nuclear warheads, and that among these warheads were 100 false, nonworking warheads. Rather than testing each one for the true and false, the Church gave all 10,000 warheads over to our enemy and said, "We just don't want to be deceived by false warheads, perhaps we will be safer by throwing out anything that looks like a warhead."

This is essentially what happens when we respond to counterfeits out of fear. If we have an attitude that says, "If anything supernatural or beyond my understanding happens, then it must be of the devil," then we have already been deceived. This perspective leaves us with no true discernment and leaves us powerless against the enemy.

We need to begin to use counterfeits as signposts. Every time a counterfeit shows up, take it as the Lord presenting you with an opportunity to reclaim the authentic from the darkness. Take up the cause to reclaim the Church's stolen property.

In the Old Testament we are told that when a thief is caught he must repay double what he stole (see Exodus 22:3-17). There is a time coming when the Church will realize that we have been robbed of our supernatural goods and that we must confront the thief. When we catch the thief (Satan), he will come face to face with the fact that he has launched the Church into double the spirituality and power that she had

Authentic vs. Counterfeit

before he robbed us. Retribution day is coming. We just have to identify the counterfeits and reclaim our stuff.

The best way to spot a counterfeit is to become an expert of the authentic. Also, when you see a counterfeit, don't shrink back in fear—let this cry rise in your heart, "THAT IS MINE, AND I WANT IT BACK!"

*This chapter is excerpted and reproduced by permission of Destiny Image Publishers from Jonathan Welton's book **Normal Christianity**, ©2011, Destiny Image Publishers.*

Go to www.heavensphysics.com/chapter5 or scan this QR code on your smartphone to share your insights and spiritual experiences about topics covered in this chapter.

51

God's New Sound is Coming

When we first considered writing this book, we wondered if others were being led on a similar journey of discovery. That's when we got the idea to find out what Christian leaders might think about our suspicion that not only is God up to something new, but this new "something" may involve sound, frequency, vibration, or energy.

We began interviewing all the leaders we could find, and were amazed to discover we weren't the only ones crazy enough to be exploring these subjects.

Every leader we interviewed had already been exploring the realms of frequencies, vibrations, and quantum physics. So we were in good company, even if we were all a little strange. You've already read what Bob Jones had to say. The following chapters share a little of what others told us they have been seeing and sensing from God.

We are very interested in what you have discovered in your own journeys into the realms of sound, light, vibrations, frequencies, energy, and quantum physics.

You can go to our website and share your insights and feedback: www.heavensphysics.com.

6

Good Vibrations
by Ellyn Davis

In 1966, The Beach Boys introduced a song called *Good Vibrations*. It quickly climbed the charts to become the #1 single in America, Great Britain and several other nations as well as the #1 Billboard Top 100 song of the year. At that time, everyone pretty much thought of "vibrations" as the kind of feeling you got from an experience or from being around another person—people, experiences or situations either gave off "good vibes" or "bad vibes."

In recent years, God has been opening the eyes of some of His people to the mysteries of sound, color and light, and of vibrations and energy.

Prophets have long recognized that their words carry a force or power that is more than just the words, but is like an "energy" that empowers what they prophesy. Some Christian leaders have also found that they have a "resonance" themselves that helps people move deeper into God.

For example, Judy Franklin has found that people who have a hard time "going to heaven" by themselves can more easily do it if they are around her, so she carries some sort of energy that helps them. Larry Randolph has always taught that proximity to someone who already operates in a particular gifting is crucial when learning to operate in that spiritual gift. And other prophets are finding that sound, color, and light have healing frequencies to them.

What if there really are "good vibrations" that God has imbedded into everything He created and we just need to be open to experiencing them? In Romans 1: 20, the Bible says that, "since the creation of the world God's invisible qualities—his eternal power and divine nature—have been clearly seen, being understood from what has been made." Could it be that there are things that we can better understand about God through things He has made such as vibrations and frequencies?

A Basic Science Lesson About Vibrations

Don't worry, you won't have to take a physics test later. However, you need to have some basic understanding of sound, light, and energy to appreciate the topics presented in the following chapters.

Physics is the branch of science concerned with discovering the nature and properties of matter and energy. Before the turn of the 20th century, physics was primarily concerned with studying matter that was generally observable to humans and how it operated.

You probably remember learning some basic physics in school and it mostly had to do with work systems (pulleys, levers, gears, etc.), objects in motion (like how fast a tennis ball falls to the ground from a two story building), and

Good Vibrations

electricity, magnetism, heat, sound, and light.

You also probably remember learning about the building blocks of matter. All matter, whether it's a daffodil, your best friend, or the remotest star, is composed of basic building blocks called atoms. And different types of atoms combine to form different types of matter.

For example, when two atoms of hydrogen combine with one atom of oxygen, a molecule of water is produced. When one atom of sodium combines with one atom of chlorine, we have what we call salt.

What if there really are "good vibrations" that God has embedded into everything He created and we just need to be open to experiencing them? Could it be that there are things that we can understand about God through things He has made such as vibrations and frequencies?

If you took the basic building block of all matter, which is the atom, and explored its smallest detectable parts, you would discover sub-atomic particles that have been given strange names like quarks and leptons and neutrinos. And if you tinkered around deeper than the sub-atomic level, you would discover even stranger entities that cannot really be called "particles" because they are more like incredibly minute packets of energy that are constantly vibrating and seem able to change from particles of matter to waves of energy (like light) and back again.

Good Vibrations

In other words, at the basic level of existence, not only is everything constantly vibrating energy, but the energy that forms the foundation of existence can manifest itself as either a particle or a wave (solid objects or invisible waves).

Waves, Vibrations, and Frequencies

When you mention "waves," most people think of the ocean, but we are surrounded by all sorts of waves all the time. Right now, wherever you are, the air around you is alive with radio waves, microwaves, TV signals, sound waves, colors, and even waves of radiation beaming down on you from the sun and beaming into you from the earth.

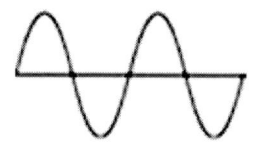

A wave is actually a series of regular vibrations in an undulating pattern like in the illustration on the left. The wavelength is the shortest distance between the peaks of each vibration. The frequency is the number of vibrations or oscillations per second.

Types of Waves

So far, scientists have identified three types of waves:

• **Mechanical waves** require a material medium like air or water to travel. One example of a mechanical wave would be the ripples created by dropping a pebble into still water. You can also create a mechanical wave by holding one end of a rope and shaking it gently until the rope makes an undulating pattern. Sound is also a mechanical wave because the sound vibrations cause the air molecules to bump against each other, creating waves of sound energy radiating out from the source of the sound, just like the dropped pebble caused the molecules of water to bump into themselves and create ripples. Sound vibrations can travel through air, water and even some solid materials.

- **Electromagnetic waves** do not require a material medium to travel. They can travel through empty space and can pass through solid matter. Light waves, radio waves, TV waves, and microwaves are examples of electromagnetic waves.
- **Matter waves** are produced by electrons and subatomic particles. In quantum mechanics, a matter wave or de Broglie wave is the wave-like behavior of subatomic particles such as electrons, pions, neutrons, and protons.

Mechanical Vibrations

The mechanical vibration we are most familiar with is sound, so let's take a look at the sound vibratory spectrum. It ranges from frequencies below the level of human hearing called infrasound to sound higher than the human ear can hear called ultrasound. Ultrasound is commonly used in medical devices for determining the outline of features deep within tissues.

Different organisms can perceive different ranges of sound frequencies. The hearing range of humans is called the audible or "acoustic" frequency sound range and it is normally limited to vibrational frequencies between approximately 6 Hz and 20,000 Hz (20 kHz). A Hertz is a measurement of the number of vibrations per second. Other species have different ranges of hearing. For example, dogs can perceive vibrations higher than 20,000 Hz, but are deaf to anything below 40 Hz.

Dolphins have the broadest range of hearing in the animal kingdom and can detect sound vibrations as low as 75 Hz and as high as 150,000 Hz.

Plants also respond to certain sound frequencies. It has been proven that specific frequencies, high tones, classical music and bird song cause plant stomata (pores) to open to receive nutrients.

Electromagnetic Vibrations

Electromagnetic vibrations differ from mechanical vibrations in several ways. First of all, electromagnetic waves do not need a medium (such as air or water) in which to travel. They can travel in a vacuum, travel through walls, and travel through outer space.

Secondly, electromagnetic vibrations consist of various forms of light and can be described in terms of a stream of photons, which are non-material light particles each traveling in a wave-like pattern and moving at the speed of light. Light is measured by its wavelength (the distance between the peaks of the vibratory waves) but sound is measured by its frequency (how many waves occur in a certain period of time). Sound is measured in hertz, light is measured in angstroms, nanometers, or electron volts.

Here are the different types of vibrations in the electromagnetic spectrum, from lowest energy to highest:

- **Radio waves**: This is the same kind of energy that radio stations, TV stations, and cell phones broadcast. Radio waves are also emitted by stars and gases in space. Radio waves have the longest wavelengths in the electromagnetic spectrum. They can be longer than a football field or as short as a football.

- **Microwaves**: You can use a microwave to heat up your left-overs, boil water and cook popcorn, but astronomers use microwaves to learn about the structure of galaxies. Microwaves are good for transmitting information from one place to another because microwave energy can penetrate haze, light rain and snow, clouds, and smoke. Microwaves are used for radar like the doppler radar used in weather forecasts. The universe also emits microwaves and we are constantly bombarded by cosmic microwave background radiation. Microwave wavelengths are in the range of a few inches.
- **Infrared**: Infrared light has a range of wavelengths, just like visible light has wavelengths that range from red to violet. "Near infrared" light is closest in wavelength to visible light and is experienced as heat. "Far infrared" is closer to the microwave region of the electromagnetic spectrum and does not emit heat The longer, far infrared wavelengths are about the size of a pin head and the shorter, near infrared ones are the size of microscopic organisms. These shorter wavelengths are the ones used by your TV's remote control. Our skin emits infrared light, which is why we can be seen in the dark by someone using night vision goggles. The Earth, the Sun, stars and galaxies also emit infrared light.
- **Visible light**: This is the only part of the electromagnetic spectrum that our eyes can see and contains all the

different colors: red, orange, yellow, green, blue, indigo and violet. Each color has a different frequency of vibration, with red having the longest vibrational frequency and violet having the shortest. When all the wavelengths of visible light are seen together, they make white light. Visible light wavelengths are about the size of microbes.

• **Ultraviolet light**: The sun emits ultraviolet (or UV) radiation that causes our skin to burn, but stars and other objects in space also emit UV radiation. Though these waves are invisible to the human eye, some insects, like bumblebees, can see them. UV wavelengths are the size of molecules.

• **X-rays**: As the wavelengths of light decrease, they increase in energy. X-rays have smaller wavelengths and therefore higher energy than ultraviolet waves. Your doctor uses X-rays to look at your bones and your dentist to look at your teeth. Many things in space emit X-rays, among them are black holes, neutron stars, binary star systems, supernova remnants, stars, the Sun, hot gases, and even some comets. The Earth's atmosphere is thick enough that virtually no X-rays are able to penetrate. X-ray wavelengths are about the size of atoms.

• **Gamma-rays**: Gamma-rays have the smallest wavelengths and the most energy of any other wave in the electromagnetic spectrum. These waves are generated by radioactive atoms and in nuclear explosions. Because gamma-rays can kill living cells, this is the type of radiation used in cancer treatment. Radioactive materials can emit gamma rays, but the biggest gamma ray generator of all is the Universe. Gamma ray wavelengths are the size of sub-atomic particles.

Good Vibrations

The only difference between the various types of electromagnetic radiation is the amount of energy found in the photons. Radio waves have photons with low energies, microwaves have a little more energy than radio waves, infrared has still more, then visible light, ultraviolet, X-rays, and, the most energetic of all, gamma-rays.

As human beings, we are only able to see about 3% of the entire light vibratory spectrum (we call it visible light) and probably only able to hear that much of the sound vibratory spectrum. This means there is a whole realm of energy and vibration we can't see with our eyes or hear with our ears. Could it be that God has given us other ways to sense the unseen and unheard?

Other Vibrational Frequencies Found in Nature

Since everything is energy at the foundational level of existence, and all energy vibrates at a certain frequency, everything that exists could be thought of as some sort of wave with its own resonant vibrational frequency.

There are many common examples of the vibrational frequencies of objects. Most of us have seen commercials or videos of a singer shattering a wine glass by singing a certain tone. This happens because the glass molecules have a particular resonant frequency and, when it is reached, the molecules begin a vibration that eventually causes the glass to shatter. There are historic examples of bridges collapsing when the cadence of soldiers marching across them matched the vibrational frequency of the bridge. That is why armies are instructed to break step when they cross bridges. In hospitals, sound is used to dissolve kidney stones by matching their resonant frequency.

Crystals also have unique frequencies. Quartz crystals have been used in watches and radios for years because of their ability to vibrate at certain frequencies. This vibration, or oscillation, is then converted into pulses suitable for the watch circuits.

There is a whole realm of energy and vibration we can't see with our eyes or hear with our ears. Could it be that God has given us other ways to sense the unseen and unheard?

Essential oils have vibrational frequencies that match and are believed to enhance the vibrational frequency of healthy cells in your body.

You may not realize it, but each part of your body has its own resonant frequency. Your brain, your heart, each organ and even your DNA has its own unique frequency. In addition, both our brain and heart emit electromagnetic fields which can change depending on our emotional and physical state.

The earth itself emits vibrations that are in the same range as the brain waves of humans and mammals. Scientists have begun to suspect that the earth's electromagnetic frequency, the Schumann Resonance, is essential to the life processes and health of organisms—particularly for humans. Fluctuations in the signal have been linked to human physical and emotional reactions, including migraine headaches, depression, suicide, the disruption of circadian rhythms, a reduction in the pineal gland output of melatonin, and increased incidences of Sudden Infant Death Syndrome.

There is growing scientific evidence that everything alive responds to subtle changes in the magnetic and electromagnetic fields surrounding us.

Future Research

We have all had the experience of interacting with someone and sensing their fear or anger or joy or of entering a room and suddenly feeling fearful or tense. We've also had incidents of synchronicity such as thinking of a person and suddenly having them call us. Many scientists are convinced those experiences indicate that thoughts and emotions, as well as words, carry vibrational frequencies that radiate into our surroundings and not only affect our own thoughts and emotions but also affect everything and everyone around us. However, no instrumentation has yet been developed to measure the vibrational frequencies of thoughts or emotions.

Although there is a great deal of conjecture as to whether the various sound, light, and other vibrational frequencies are interrelated, very little scientific research has been done to develop correlations between the vibrations that surround us and to determine how they may affect our lives and health.

Go to www.heavensphysics.com/chapter6 or scan this QR code on your smartphone to share your insights and spiritual experiences about topics covered in this chapter.

Human Brainwaves

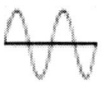

Our brain emits brainwaves which can change in vibrational frequency depending on our emotional and physical states.

There are four common categories of these brainwaves, ranging from the most activity to the least activity. When the brain is aroused, alert and engaged in heightened mental activity, it generates *beta* brainwaves with a frequency between 14 and 30 Hz. At the highest levels of *beta*, a person's mind may race and he may become agitated and tense.

In the *alpha* brainwave state, we are usually in a state of physical and mental relaxation. The *alpha* state is the ideal condition to learn new information. *Alpha* brainwaves are associated with serotonin release and enhanced immunity. They vibrate at a frequency of 8 to 13 Hz.

Theta brainwaves occur in a state where tasks become so automatic that you can mentally disengage from them. *Theta* is typically a very positive mental state and can sometimes be trancelike. *Theta* brainwave frequencies are between 4 and 8 Hz.

The final brainwave state is *delta*, with vibrations of 0.1 to 4 Hz. Typically a person is asleep during the *delta* state although people who have practiced mediation for long periods of time can achieve *delta* while fully conscious.

7

Sound of Heaven Symphony of Earth
by Ray Hughes

There is much we don't know yet about sound and its relationship to the unveiling of God's glory. In this chapter Ray Hughes shares how God released heavenly sounds each time He interacted with mankind in a significant way and He has created each of us to make a unique "sound" that reflects His glory on earth.

We live in the "Information Age," an age of increasing revelation, prophetic insight and sensitivity to the spirit realm. There is certainly no shortage of intellectual stimulation, and spirituality has become almost a flippant byword in some circles, we live in a time when science fiction can become science fact overnight.

The more I researched and mined the truths about sound, the more I realized there is much we don't yet know about sound and its relationship to the unveiling of God's glory. Although I am neither a scientist nor an educator, I enjoy and take advantage of scientific information. I believe that the Holy Spirit has given me some of the pieces of the puzzle to heaven's sound, so the information I share with you about sound and light and vibration will be based on scientific fact, confessed speculation, and spiritual revelation.

Sound Truths

The day God chose to create light was the day music began. Light and sound travel through the medium of waves. Moving light waves are called electromagnetic waves. The wavelength of an electromagnetic wave determines which type of wave it is. As humans, we're only able to see 3 percent of the entire light spectrum, and part of the 97 percent of invisible light is categorized as electromagnetic waves. Within electromagnetic light exists a range of wavelengths called radio waves. Within this category of radio waves exists an even smaller range of waves that humans can hear.

Essentially, we know that these categories and forms of light and sound fall within the same spectrum. The first time God said, "Let there be light," (Genesis 1:3), He was also proclaiming the beginning of sound.

When He said, "light," it was heard in the sea of void and darkness. In reality, He was releasing the light of His glory.

Remember, the sun and moon were not created until the fourth day, so this light was the light of His glory. In this instant, music was born. Although light and sound are located on different frequencies, they are the same thing. The Bible says, "God is light, and in Him there is no darkness at all" (I John 1:5 NAS). Everything that God has ever brought forth has come from His creative voice—the same voice which impregnates the earth with light, sound, music and glory, the elements of God.

Sound of Heaven

The sound of heaven that is called the "sound of many waters" in Revelation 14: 2, encompasses all the frequencies in the sound spectrum. The four universal elements are water, wind, fire, and earth. The sound of heaven—all the frequencies of the sound spectrum—can be heard in water, wind, and fire. We are made of the fourth element which is dirt. God desires for that same sound to be heard through the earth. When He created us, He simply animated dirt. Imagine the first sound Adam ever heard was God breathing the wind or the breath of His Spirit.

The first time God said, "Let there be light," He was also proclaiming the beginning of sound.

We are the only ones made in His image. We are the creatures God chose to give free will to accept or reject His sound breathing in us. The wind does not have a will, and neither does fire nor water. Man has been given a will, because man has been given a soul. Therefore, we have a choice to align our sound with the sound of heaven, while the other elements remain inanimate. Fire simply sounds like fire, wind sounds like wind, and water sounds like water. Man sounds like man, but we have been given the creative ability to release the sound of God.

Sound is an amazing force. A pair of 30 inch speakers connected to a tone generator can generate a note powerful enough to move a building off its foundation.

Sound of Heaven

We cannot begin to understand sound until we realize that we are unable to hear most of the sounds that exist. We are continually in the presence of ultrasonic and subsonic sound waves. "Ultra," which means "above," are sound waves above our threshold of hearing. "Sub," which means "beneath," are waves beneath our threshold of hearing. Just because we don't see the wind doesn't mean it's not there. Just because we don't hear a sound does not mean it was never made.

Sight and Sound

Sound has the power to change everything. Imagine a scene from a movie where a woman is walking down a sidewalk in a busy city on a fall afternoon. The street is crowded with business people on their lunch break. The wind is picking up, making the dead leaves swirl around her feet with every step. The woman, in her forties, is wearing a navy blue skirt and a white blouse and her right hand is clutching the strap of her purse as she walks extremely fast. From these visuals, what do we know about the situation? Very little.

Now take the same scene and add the eerie sound of a lonely, faint chime and a futuresque dissonant chord from a synthesizer. Add the boom of a bass drum playing sporadically as if in a death march. Now we feel something. We're scared for the woman because the background sound gives us the impression that something bad is going to happen to her.

Change the music to a light piccolo playing over the staccato plucks of an orchestra's violin section and the scene becomes more playful and we imagine a happier reason why she might be in a hurry. Finally, change the music to the slow, lush sound of strings passionately playing a love song and our hearts drop as we wonder is she is hurrying to get to a hospital where her love is dying.

Sound can create a story from dry facts. It causes our emotions to go beyond facts to feelings. The facts' meaning depends entirely on how the viewer or listener chooses to respond emotionally, and that meaning can also depend on their mood while watching and listening. The revelation that comes to the seer has everything to do with the sound of the scene being viewed.

The woman walking is a picture of the church progressively taking steps forward, often frantically. The sound being heard as the church moves forward has everything to do with how the seers will interpret what goes on. Therefore, the sound impacts how they will pray, how they will believe, and how they will interpret the activity they see in the church. Are they walking into a season of peace, a season of death, a season of being raped and violated by the world?

Music is the indicator. Sound sets the tone for her destiny. Throughout the generations of history, the spiritual climate of God's people has always responded to a musical indicator.

With every revival, there has been a release of new music or new sound. Whether the music releases revival, or whether the revival releases the music varies from generation to generation. However, the sound changes as God's people respond to what God is doing and saying.

I know we could argue that sound and music continually change as a result of the development of the technology of any given generation. But the fact is, God gives the technology also. It's a chicken or egg deal. Any way you look at it, God unveils new songs and new sounds in relationship to the new revelation of His presence in His people.

Sound has always been and always will be one of the most important forces God ever created. It can calm our souls at the side of a brook as we hear water trickling over small stones. It can utterly frighten us in an instant as a tray of dishes is dropped in a restaurant. Sound can soothe the weary mind to a place of sleep and rest. Sound can cause the earth to convulse in the form of an earthquake.

Sound has always been and always will be one of the most important forces God ever created.

An earthquake is nothing more than sound modulation between two layers of stone formations that come together miles under the earth. Windows can be blown out of your house as an airplane overhead breaks the sound barrier. Nerves can be put on edge at the monotonous drip of a faucet.

Man can be motivated by a patriotic song to give his life for his country. Man can be motivated by enticing words to betray a Godly marriage and carry out lustful and sinful acts.

We can swell with pride at the sound of an anthem being played as our sons and daughters walk down the aisle with tasseled caps. We can be jolted into action at the sound of a fire alarm or we can be lulled to sleep at the whisper of a breeze.

Is there a particular anointing on instruments or sounds today that will give us the upper hand on our enemies? *Yes and no.* Yes, because particular sounds, tones, and frequencies motivate us to particular responses. And no, because an instrument does not have a life of its own. It is an inanimate object.

Water and Thunder

Revelation 19:6 refers to the "sound of many waters" and of "mighty thunderings." That's the sound of corporate worship in heaven. For us to understand what that sounds like, think of 10,000 Niagara Falls. Think of 250,000 people in the Super Dome, multiplied 250,000 times and every person releasing every ounce of their energy, body, soul, and spirit in an explosive expression of worship unto God. It sounds like white noise, or the sound of many waters. The fact is, that's what it sounds like in heaven.

Though it can vary from person to person, God created us with the ability to hear in the range of between 16 and 20,000 Hertz. That is 16 vibrations per second up to 16,000 vibrations per second. When I hit an "A" note on the piano, your eardrum vibrates at 440 times per second. That's what makes it an "A" note. When you go up a note, your eardrum vibrates more times per second. When you go down a note, it vibrates fewer times per second.

If the entire sound spectrum were represented by a graph three feet wide, humans could only hear three-fourths of an inch of that entire spectrum. That's a huge portion of sound that we never hear because it's either above or below the human auditory threshold. It's like a dog whistle. When we blow a dog whistle, we don't hear it. But a dog can because his eardrums are created to vibrate at a higher frequency than ours.

An oscilloscope is a device created to detect and determine sound frequencies. If you set an oscilloscope beside Niagara Falls, you will discover that there are sounds within the sound of the falls that are beyond what an oscilloscope can measure.

Our invented devices to capture the unheard and unseen things on earth are limited. In heaven, however, there are no limitations. There, twenty four hours a day, the sound of many waters rolls from the throne and into the throne room.

When the sound of many waters, which is the song of the Lord, comes illuminating out of heaven and joins the realm that we are living in, phenomenal things happen. Take a look at the shepherds on the night Jesus was born. The angel of the Lord appeared in a massive blast of light of the glory of the Lord and suddenly, a multitude of angelic voices started singing, "Hallelujah!" The sound of heaven came to earth.

This same glory appeared earlier when Solomon was dedicating the temple. II Chronicles 5: 11 – 14 tells us that when the musicians and singers were in unison praising God, the house of the Lord was filled with a cloud so heavy that the priests could not continue ministering. And John had a similar encounter in Revelations 19:6 that he describes as hearing "the sound of a great multitude, and as the sound of many waters, and as the sound of mighty thundering."

The sound of heaven was heard in the temple during its dedication and during the night of King Jesus' birth. When was the next time we experienced this sound? In Acts 2, the disciples went to the upper room and did just as was done in the Old Testament. In II Chronicles 5, the people lifted up their voices "as one." In Acts when the sound of heaven suddenly visited earth again, "they were all with one accord in one place" (Acts 2: 1).

The sound came when that true unity—God unity—was there. The real unity. Every time the sound of many waters visited earth, the entire generation was impacted. I believe with my whole heart that God is doing something now that is so dynamic the entire next generation is going to experience it.

When the sound of heaven is magnified by the creative force of God releasing His authority to the Earth, the sound of corporate worship is heard. It is the sound of many waters and the sound of mighty thunder. In Revelation 14: 2, John even heard these sounds of heaven combined with the "sound of harpists playing their harps."

Every time that sound visited the Earth something phenomenal took place. When the sound that resonates out of the heart of God's people comes into agreement with the sound resonating out of God's heart, we find worship on earth as it is in heaven.

To experience the worship of heaven is one of God's greatest desire for our lives.

Sound of Heaven

A Glorified Sound

Have you ever thought about why there's such a difference between a guitar and a trumpet? Or how about a trumpet and a cornet? What makes a trumpet sound like a trumpet and a cornet sound like a cornet? It all has to do with the vibrations reflecting off different pieces of matter in the instrument. The vibrations coming out of a trumpet are different from those coming out of a cornet. They have a different rate, frequency or even length. Therefore, a rounder, softer sound out of a trumpet and a higher, more direct sound from a cornet occurs.

The sound produced from an instrument has everything to do with the size and texture of the material of the instrument from which it's reflecting. Every instrument ever made is unique, for it contains its own sound. Sound through God's creation becomes individual and therefore, dependent upon the instrument. With our hope for glory—Christ dwelling in us—we produce a sound that's been in us since the beginning of time. We bring to life the full meaning of Emmanuel—Christ with us, Christ revealed in us. "Then it was revealed in my hearing by the Lord of hosts." Christ will be revealed as we hear His sound and release our individual, God-appointed sound as His unique instruments.

"Christ in you, the hope of glory" (Colossians 1: 27). The word "glory" means "lightified." From this, we can deduce that Christ in you is the hope of being "lit," or the hope of being "sounded." Christ is your hope of producing the sound that has resided in you since the beginning of time. Your sole purpose of existence as a worshiper of God is to be the personal instrument He created you to be, and played for His glory. With the very truth of the living Christ is the assurance you will be played before God.

I Corinthians 2: 9 – 10 says, "Eye has not seen nor ear heard, nor have entered into the heart of man the things which God has prepared for those who love Him. But God has revealed them to us through His Spirit. For the Spirit searches all things, yes, the very things of God." As we talk about the sound of heaven it's essential to understand that our eyes have not seen and our ears have not heard. Our soulish eyes and ears cannot take in the truth of God. But it is His Spirit within us, Emmanuel, that reveals. God desires to release a sound that our personal issues cannot resist.

The sound God desires to release will chase religion from the church and bring truth. He desires the sound of many waters, the sound of mighty thunders, and the sound of His glory and authority in the church.

*This chapter is excerpted with permission from Ray Hughes' book **Sound of Heaven, Symphony of Earth**.*

Go to www.heavensphysics.com/chapter7 or scan this QR code on your smartphone to share your insights and spiritual experiences on topics covered in this chapter.

The Power of Sound

For thousands of years, different cultures throughout the world have recognized that sound vibrations affect both human consciousness and the physical body. There are historical records of Islamic, Chinese, Hebrew, Egyptian and Greek cultures using sound to instill cultural wisdom, create altered states of consciousness and heal the sick.

In ancient Greece, Plato and Aristotle taught their students that illnesses often were a result of a disharmonious state of being—a discordant resonant frequency—and they saw music as a primary means of reestablishing a healthy resonance. The term "resonate" literally means "return to sound." Music was used to "tune" the body to its natural "sound," its natural resonant frequency.

In Christian tradition, music has also been considered to have healing powers. Many of the great cathedrals in Europe were designed to be harmonic resonating chambers for sound and music to heal, amplify, and alter consciousness during worship and prayer. And Gregorian chants were based on the Solfeggio frequencies, special tones believed to have transformative power and impart spiritual blessings.

8

The God Vibration
by Dan McCollam

Modern scientific discoveries have recently joined the voice of ancient sacred writings to pull back the veil of ignorance that once shrouded the power of sound in God's universe. Today these applied sciences and theologies can be woven together towards the redemptive understanding of sounds that heal, deliver, destroy, and open up portals in the heavenly realms. This chapter shares a little of Dan McCollam's insights about the amazing power that God has hidden for us in sound.

Quantum physics serves as one of the great scientific disciplines bridging the river of confusion between science and biblical kingdom thinking. One of the basic tenants of quantum physics states that the universe is in a constant state of vibratory motion. Simply put, everything has a vibration at the center of it. The chair you are sitting in right now is vibrating. Your body vibrates. The book you are holding resonates with vibrations. Yes, the whole universe, according to quantum physics, is filled with vibrations.

String and superstring theories agree with this basic tenet. String theory originated as a modern mathematical approach to theoretical physics. But, like quantum physics, the theory claims that tiny vibrating strands of energy compose and connect all matter. Does the Bible give any evidence to support the idea that vibration is at the center of created matter? If so, what is it? And where did it come from? I believe the answers to these questions can be found in the first three verses of Genesis.

> *Everything has a vibration at the center of it. The chair you are sitting in right now is vibrating. The book you are holding resonates with vibrations. Yes, the whole universe, according to quantum physics, is filled with vibrations.*

Let's Begin "In The Beginning"

Genesis 1: 1-3 says, "In the beginning God created the heavens and the earth. Now the earth was formless and empty, darkness was over the surface of the deep, and the Spirit of God was hovering over the waters. And God said, 'Let there be light,' and there was light.'"

At first glance the beginning three verses of Genesis may seem a bit contradictory. In verse one, for instance, God creates the heavens and the earth, but in verse two it appears that the earth and heavens have no form, shape or definition. Later in the Genesis account we find that the sky (or heavens) and dry ground (earth) were created on days two and three. So which is it? Did God create the heavens and the earth formless, empty, and dark then improve upon it later?

The writings of the late Dr. Henry Morris, founder of the Creation Research Institute were very helpful to me in clarifying this seeming contradiction. Dr. Morris believed that the first three verses of Genesis represented three distinct activities of the Godhead in the work of creation. Let me see if I can explain it in simplified terms.

Divine Partnership In Creation

First, God the Father created the nuclear matter or atomic particles that would be necessary for the formation of everything pertaining to the heavens and the earth. This act demonstrates the awesome and unique power of God to create something out of nothing.

The writer of Hebrews puts it this way, "By faith we understand that the universe was formed at God's command, so that what is seen was not made out of what was visible." (Hebrews 11:3) According to Genesis the earth was still "formless and empty" at this point in the creation process. God had created the particles of matter that would be used to shape his ultimate intention of the heavens and the earth, but it did not yet look like the heavens and earth we know today.

Next, the Holy Spirit moved or hovered over the atomic particles referred to in Genesis as the "formless and empty" earth. The word interpreted as "hovered", "moved" or "brooded" in our translations is the word "rachaph" in the original Hebrew, which in modern scientific terms could be defined as "vibrated." Therefore it could be said that the Holy Spirit vibrated over the formless universe. Vibrations are the forces that hold particle matter together. Light waves, sound waves, and electromagnetic waves released by the "God vibration" enabled the particle matter of the universe to take on specific physical form.

Now that sound waves existed, Jesus the Word was able to speak form and shape to the nuclear matter. Whatever Jesus the Word spoke took on the shape and form of his command. "'And God said, 'Let there be light' and there was light.'" (Genesis 1:3) This partnership in creation between the Father and Son is recognized in the writings of John, "In the beginning was the Word, and the Word was with God, and the Word was God. He was with God in the beginning. Through him all things were made; without him nothing was made that has been made." (John 1:1-3)

If anyone has any question that John is speaking about Jesus, he clarifies it further in verse ten by saying, "He was in the world, and though the world was made through him, the world did not recognize him."

John clearly states here that Jesus made the world in partnership with the Father. The Holy Spirit is not mentioned in John's text because John's purpose is to exalt Christ as the pre-existent Son of God.

Still, the Genesis account makes it clear that all three persons of the Trinity were involved in the creation process.

The three-way partnership between the Father, Son and Holy Spirit may also be represented in God's statement concerning the creation of man. "Then God said, 'Let us make man in our image, in our likeness...'" (Genesis 1:26) God's choice of the pronouns "us" and "our" in the context of his creative process further supports the evidence of a divine three-way partnership in creation.

Perhaps now we have answered one of our questions, "Where did the vibration come from?"

Energy does not create itself; it must have a source or energizer. Movement does not exist without causative forces; there must be a prime mover. Genesis has provided reasonable evidence to conclude that God not only created matter but also started the vibrations at the center of it.

Though all these types of waves are invisible, the book of Colossians includes the invisible realm in its description of creation, It says in Colossians 1:16-17, "For by him were all things created, that are in heaven, and that are in earth, visible and invisible, ...all things were created by him and for him. And he is before all things, and by him all things consist." The Colossians reference to the invisible created realm speaks specifically of the spiritual dimension but could certainly include these vibrational forces.

Let's put the pieces of this sound puzzle together.

Physicists claim that the universe is in a constant state of vibratory motion. String theory claims that there are tiny vibrating strands of energy at the center of all matter. Genesis and the leading authority on creation research tell us that the Holy Spirit vibrated over nuclear matter to energize it, giving it the ability to be shaped and formed. Colossians tells us that God created all visible and invisible things and that, "...By Him all things consist."

Are you seeing the picture? All created things vibrate and the Creator initiated this vibration in the Genesis account of creation.

Quantum Field Theory

Let's add another piece to our sound puzzle.

Dr. John Beaulieu is a psychologist, musician, and practitioner of naturopathic medicine who has proposed an interesting application of quantum field theory. Quantum field theory, as Dr. Beaulieu applies it, suggests that the quantum field in a scientific experiment is more significant than its manifestation. Simply put, the cause is greater than the effect it produces.

If one were to apply this principle to vibration and creation you might say that created matter is only the response to a greater field, in this case a vibration.

Cathy Guzetta, in the book, *Music Therapy: Nursing the Music of the Soul*, proposes that trees, plants, rocks, and people are perhaps music that has taken on visible form. Assuming the application of this theory has merit, one would be led to ask, "Where then is the voice or music coming from that shapes creation?"

C. S. Lewis must have imagined a similar concept in his acclaimed children's fiction, *The Magician's Nephew*, from his *Chronicles of Narnia* series. Here, Lewis pictures the great lion Aslan singing Narnia into existence. Polly and Digory are two young children who watch in amazement as everything the lion sings takes on the shape, character, and color of his song.

The God Vibration

Now it's quite obvious that C.S. Lewis was writing children's fiction, not establishing quantum theory or systematic theology, but Beaulieu's principle and Lewis's fiction could easily make one wonder if all that we see and enjoy in creation is simply a visible form of the "Lion's song."

> *Trees, plants, rocks, and people are perhaps music that has taken on visible form. Where then is the voice or music coming from that shapes creation? It makes one wonder if all that we see and enjoy in creation is simply a visible form of the "Lion's song."*

Holding The Universe Together

Not only does it appear that there is certainly a vibration at the center of all creation, but that same vibrating strand may be what holds the universe together.

We know from the Genesis account that God spoke creation into existence, but according to the book of Hebrews, His powerful word is still what is holding the universe together. "The Son is the radiance of God's glory and the exact representation of his being, sustaining all things by his powerful word." (Hebrews 1:3)

I believe that the string or vibration at the center of all matter in the universe is in fact the sound wave from the word God spoke over each created thing at its entry into existence. His voice, that God vibration, is the glue holding all creation together. Colossians 1:17 states, "He is before all things, and in him all things hold together."

The words that God speaks live forever and supersede our material reality. "Heaven and earth will pass away but my words will never pass away." (Luke 21:33)

Like the quantum field theory we examined earlier, we see that God's words shape physical matter but the words themselves are a greater reality than what they create because they "never pass away." This is why scripture says that God cannot lie.

Not only is it against God's holy nature and character to speak something that is untrue, it is actually physically impossible for him to lie because whatever God speaks simply is. If God spoke something it could not be a lie because the nanosecond God's word proceeds from his mouth it exists in both the material and spiritual dimensions.

Therefore, it is impossible for God to lie both in the integrity of his divine nature and by material fact that whatever he speaks already is.

All Creation Sings

"Praise him, sun and moon, praise him, all you shining stars... Praise the Lord from the earth" (Psalm 148:3,7)

Everything in the universe has a vibration at the center of it. Nothing in the universe exists without motion or vibration and every vibration makes a sound. Therefore, it can be rightly said that all creation is truly singing.

Most of us are aware that every individual on the planet

has a unique DNA blueprint (except identical twins.) Your DNA, or deoxyribonucleic acid, is composed of long strings of molecules called nucleotides that represent themselves in a sequence of dozens of unique combinations.

Since the formula for your DNA can be converted to a logical alphanumeric sequence it can also be transformed into musical notes. In other words, your DNA is an original song!

In the 1990's, Susan Alexander, professor of music in Sacramento, California teamed up with Dr. David Deemer of the University of California. Together they collaborated to create a musical composition of Alexander's DNA so that the concept of a life song could actually be heard. Since then many other forms of DNA have been musically encoded.

Increasing Our Vibrational Sensitivity

As noted earlier, all of creation is constantly resonating with the praises of God. (Psalm 19:1-4) God's voice and the sound of angels can also be heard and experienced by man. A whole new realm of encounter awaits those who possess three simple qualities: expectancy, intentionality, and intimacy. Because God, creation, and the angels are constantly interacting, we can expect to hear them at times.

But how can we begin hearing more? How can we increase our sensitivity to the sounds of God in whatever form they appear?

Open your heart, your eyes, and your ears with an expectancy to encounter the sounds and sights of heaven on a new level. Don't limit your future level of potential for spiritual encounter by your past experience. God wants to broadband

The God Vibration

your ability to receive from Him. He delights in interacting with his children. Faith and expectancy create an environment for encounter.

Intentionality as it applies to vibrational sensitivity is simply the decision to see and to listen.

No more passive seeing or hearing. Activate your sensitivity to your aural and spiritual environment. When you suspect a unique sound or light encounter—follow it. Track it down with questions and interaction with the Holy Spirit.

Finally, encounters are born out of intimacy. Keep your heart tender and humble in seeking the Lord. At the slightest impression of the Lord's calling turn aside to meet with Him even if just for a moment.

Cultivate a sense of the Lord's presence in your everyday life. Take time to let your heart go out to him even when your attention is divided with other responsibilities. Intimacy is the incubator of increased encounters from the supernatural realm.

This chapter is excerpted with permission from Dan McCollam's manuscript **God Vibrations**.

Go to www.heavensphysics.com/chapter8 or scan this QR code on your smartphone to share your insights and spiritual experiences on topics covered in this chapter.

Cymatics

The 18th century German physicist and musician Ernst Chladni first demonstrated a way to make sound vibrations visible. When he drew a violin bow around the edge of a plate covered with sand, the sand formed intricate geometric patterns which today are termed "Chladni figures." (Examples of Chladni figures are found above and below.)

In the 1960's Dr. Hans Jenny duplicated much of Chaldni's work and investigated the three-dimensional effects of sound vibrations by placing materials like sand, spores, iron filings, mercury, water, and gases on vibrating plates or membranes. Using simple tones within audible range, Jenny was able to produce beautiful geometric shapes, spirals, and wave-like patterns.

Jenny pointed out the resemblance between the shapes and patterns we see around us and the shapes and patterns he generated with sound and became convinced that everything that exists is the result of vibrations, and that the nature of the vibration determines the ultimate form. He speculated that every cell has its own frequency, and as embryos develop, cells with harmonious frequencies form organs. He also suspected that disease is a result of inharmonious frequencies in the body.

Jenny eventually invented a cymatic instrument (from the Greek word "kymatica," meaning "pertaining to waves") that allowed him to create 3 dimensional physical images of various sounds, including human vowels and tones. He observed that the moving 3 dimensional shapes and formations composed by different sounds created precise geometric patterns.

When the vowels of ancient sacred languages such as Hebrew, Sanskrit, Egyptian, and Tibetan were pronounced, the vibration took the shape of the written symbols for these vowels, while our modern languages failed to produce the same result. Jenny concluded that, by sounding sacred texts and singing sacred vowels in these ancient languages, it is possible to transform physical reality by using sound to change its molecular structure.

An interesting fact is that some crop circles duplicate the patterns Jenny created with sound, which has led scientists to theorize that crop circles may be formed by sound frequency anomalies.

9

Angelic Encounters
by Cal Pierce

Cal Pierce's interest in sound, light, and vibrations began with an angelic encounter. Here is his account of that encounter.

Several years ago, I began asking the Lord about the energy crisis. I knew there had to be a Kingdom answer to the energy crisis. A few months later I went to a meeting where Tim Sheets taught about angels and shared Psalm 91, "He sends his angels to render service on behalf of those who inherit salvation." I discovered that the word "render service" means to "run errands." I was really stirred by the idea that God sends angels to run errands on our behalf.

At the end of that meeting an apostolic leader spoke and said, "God is beginning to release Kingdom building codes." From my experience with construction, I know about building codes so I wondered what this might mean. As soon as the session ended, I looked up to see an angel standing right in front of me. I'm not an angel type of guy, but suddenly there was an angel speaking to me saying, "I'm sent by God to answer your question about the energy crisis. I am the energy angel." All I could think was, "What on earth did I have for breakfast?"

The angel went with me back to my hotel room and began talking to me about energy. He told me that if we continue to draw resources from the planet, from this earth, we'll pollute the environment and the resources will eventually run out. But if we draw resources from above, they'll never pollute the planet and they will never run out. Then he said, "I want to show you the water car."

I said, "The what?"

He replied, "The water car. I'll be right back."

He promptly disappeared and I was left thinking, "What happened? Where did he go? Do I have a forgetful angel?" As soon as I thought that, the angel returned. He had a scroll and said, "This is the water car," as he unrolled the scroll. On the scroll was the blueprint for a vehicle. It had no engine, drive line, or transmission. Instead it had a tank and electrodes and a water container and some sort of closed system that linked them all together.

I couldn't understand the blueprint and said, "I'm not an engineer." The angel replied, "Well, I am. I'm going to show you how energy can be produced with water and light. I will come alongside you and show you more details about the water car and you'll get more information as time goes by because I'm going to connect you with people who will help you."

It was a nice day outside, so I asked the angel if he wanted to take a walk with me. His answer was, "I've been walking with you for 30 years but you just didn't know it." We went outside and walked around for awhile and he shared how water produces energy and about Niagara Falls and how we can use water to produce power. He said, "Fast water will equal energy. Let me show you how water can be moved fast with light." I replied, "I'm amazed. I'm walking with an angel." He looked at me and said, "I'm amazed too." I asked, "Why would you be amazed?" and he said, "I'm amazed because I've been trying to get your attention for 30 years."

When I got back to my room I wrote four pages of notes about everything the angel shared with me.

Sound, Light, and Energy

That angel's visit started me on an adventure in learning more about sound, light, and energy. I began sharing with people, "There's something the angel is about to reveal that has to do with sound. It's a revelation about how to produce power with sound. Sound will literally drive vehicles and produce the power to drive the planet. Because God, in Genesis used sound. He released a sound that had so much power in it that it became creative."

I later met a man God had taken to heaven and shown how to produce four dimensional objects with sound. This man told me he has used sound to project a house that is 2 1/2 inches square and is three dimensional so you can walk around and look inside the windows. He said, "I'm about to enlarge the house to 18 inches." That was my first encounter with the creative power of sound.

Later, I attended a conference where I heard a Native American share about sonoluminescence—sounds creating bursts of light. When intense waves of sound are applied to a liquid, bubbles form that collapse with such force that light is produced. The vibrations of the sound in the liquid cause a luminescence that has enough power to melt steel.

I already knew that light and water could produce energy but hadn't been sure what the relationship with sound was. But after hearing that talk on sonoluminescence, I really pressed in to discover how sound fits in with the water car.

The Power of the Spoken Word

God began to teach me through this angel about sound and the power of the spoken word. He said that because God spoke His creative will, man can also speak words that create. God's Word produces faith and faith is the substance of something, the evidence of something not seen, but it is activated by sound.

There's a reason why God's Word is living and active and it will not return void. What makes it not return void? Angels. Psalm 91 tells us that God sends His angels to render service on behalf of those who inherit salvation, or to run errands, and Psalm 103:20, says, "My angels, mighty in God, who obey the sound of His word." So when you get the will or word of God in you, you have something in you of God that is creative. When the creator releases a word, the word itself becomes creative.

Angels obey the sound of His word. When we speak His word, angels then take what we say to completion. They render service, or run errands, on behalf of those who inherit salvation, and they are waiting to for us to speak the sound of God's word so that they can take it out to accomplish what He has sent it to do. It's our partnering with the angels and angelic activity that is going to cause sound to become creative. Angels are around you to activate the revelation of the truth that you speak out into its creative form.

That's why faith requires a confession—so that it can be heard. Because those angels don't know what you're thinking, they're waiting to hear what you're saying. So, as we speak out the word that God has given us, angels will begin to bring it to completion and it will no longer go out void.

Angels don't know what you're thinking but they know what you're saying. That's why the Word requires a sound. When God speaks, worlds come in to being. What He speaks is alive and carries with it the power for its fulfillment.

This chapter is adapted from an interview with Cal Pierce.

Please share with us if you have had an angelic encounter in which you received instructions for a new invention or were given a new insight. You can scan this QR code in your smartphone or go directly to the website at www.heavensphysics.com/chapter9 to share your experiences.

The Schumann Resonance

The earth emits electromagnetic vibrations in the same frequency range as the brainwaves of humans in a relaxed mental state (alpha brainwave state). This vibration is called the Schumann Resonance and it is sometimes called "the heartbeat of mother earth."

In a study by Professor R. Wever from the Max Planck Institute for Behavioral Physiology, volunteers who spent four weeks in an underground bunker that completely screened out this vibration became disoriented and suffered emotional distress and migraine headaches. After only a brief exposure to the Schumann Resonance, the volunteers' symptoms disappeared.

The same complaints were reported by the first astronauts and cosmonauts in space. Now modern spacecraft contain a device which simulates the Schumann Resonance.

Because of this research, some scientists are concerned that all of the different man made electromagnetic waves (such as microwaves, TV and radio waves, and cellphones) that now fill our atmosphere are drowning out the Schumann Resonance. Some believe this vibration is like a natural tuning fork, not just for the oscillators of the human brain but for all processes of life.

10

Spiritual Synesthesia
by Larry Randolph

In Ephesians 1: 18-19, Paul writes, "I pray that the eyes of your heart may be enlightened in order that you may know the hope to which he has called you, the riches of his glorious inheritance in his holy people, and his incomparably great power for us who believe." In this chapter, written from an interview, Larry Randolph explains why preparing for what is to come may mean learning to interact with God in many more ways than we ever imagined.

God's New Sound

I believe we are on the verge of experiencing Pentecost on a new level and in a new measure. Time and again the prophets have declared that "something is coming," and our hearts are filled with expectation to receive all that God has for us. Even so, we still await the "fullness" of what we know is possible in God—a "fullness of Pentecost" for which the original Pentecost provided the down payment.

Though I welcome these declarations, what we really need is to experience something beyond the realm of mere proclamation. We need to see and experience God with all of our spiritual, emotional, and physical senses. We need to be impacted with the same kind of "sound" from heaven that penetrated the atmosphere on the day of Pentecost. I'm weary of sermons and teachings that only restate our need for transformation. What I'm hungry for is to experience something fresh from heaven. Now! Not later!

> *I believe we are on the verge of experiencing Pentecost on a new level and in a new measure.*

For several years, I have been praying about the purpose of this "new sound" and what it might look like. Recently, I've come to believe that certain aspects of this "heavenly sound" might be like Genesis 1, when God spoke into the void of space. The sound of His voice was so powerful, in fact, that it caused the universe to roar into existence at the speed of light. Through the "sound" of God's voice, divine energy was released, splitting the atoms and forming a heaven and earth suitable for the habitation of created man. Not long afterwards, this created man, Adam, also heard the sound of God's voice in the Garden, beckoning him to a deeper relationship with his Creator.

All this tells me that a divine sound from heaven, or at least the sound of God's voice, can cause mind-boggling phenomena to happen. In the case of Adam, hearing the sound of God's voice was merely an invitation into a deeper realm of supernatural experience. That which began as a sound, apparently, led to multiple expressions of seeing, feeling, sensing, and communicating with the Creator.

Recently, I've been pondering the similarities between the sound of God's voice in Genesis and the sound of a heavenly wind on the day of Pentecost in Acts. I began to realize that just as the sound of God's voice to Adam was merely an introduction into other realms of encountering God, those in the upper room also heard a sound that opened them up to other realms of supernatural phenomena. What they heard caused them to see fiery tongues, which caused them to feel drunk, which, in turn, caused them to speak in a heavenly language. So, the sound of wind they initially heard seemed completely unrelated to what they saw, experienced, and released.

Sound Experiences

With this in mind, I began to research the different experiences sound can cause. I quickly discovered that in psychology there is a dynamic called "synesthesia." Recent studies show that synesthesia affects 3-4% of the world's population. Synesthesia, meaning "to perceive together," causes a person's neural pathways to be cross-wired in such a way that their five senses interact with each other. This unusual mingling of their senses allows them to hear colors, smell numbers, taste sound, and so forth.

Considering the description of Pentecost in the book of Acts, it appears that a spiritual synesthesia of sorts happened on that day. The bottom line is they heard a "sound" like a mighty rushing wind that lead to a number of other different experiences. As stated, the 120 in the upper room

Spiritual Synesthesia

heard a sound, which caused them to see something, which caused them to feel something, which caused them to release something.

So, how can hearing a sound of a wind create such a unique chain reaction? Again, the answer is clear: a heavenly "sound" can create a heightened level of synesthesia that opens our senses to extreme encounters with the supernatural. As a result, we are enabled to experience God with every fiber of our being.

Moving Beyond the Familiar

Many believers today religiously cling to familiar interpretations of spiritual phenomena. If they were to hear a sound like a rushing wind, for example, the temptation would be to preach about that manifestation in hopes of evoking an even greater sound from Heaven. This inability to stretch their capacity to see and feel beyond what they actually hear often limits the scope of their experience in God.

However, if sound is vibrational, then we must understand that it can stimulate our other senses. What if the men and women at Pentecost had only embraced what they heard? It's possible that they would have missed God altogether. Instead, after hearing a new sound, they were willing to allow that sound to cause a synesthetic response in them. Through this cross-wiring of their spiritual senses, the neural pathways of the spirit realm created a myriad of spiritual encounters.

This is the kind of heavenly sound for which I've been longing. It's a new sound that will trigger our senses to "hear" what we see and "see" what we hear. As a consequence, we will "hear" outside of the realm of just a vibration on our eardrum. We will experience the sound of heaven with our whole spirit, emotions, and physical body. The result will be a fresh expression of Pentecost.

Why is this so important? I believe the more our senses are involved in receiving from Heaven, the more of God's Spirit we will retain. In this next move of the Spirit, I am convinced that our encounter with God will radically transform the realm of our senses. This will be the second Pentecost—hearing something from Heaven; seeing something different than what we heard; feeling something different than what we saw and heard; and releasing something totally different from what we saw, heard, and felt.

In light of this truth, we need to start training ourselves to hear from God with our entire being. No longer should we limit the way we "receive," nor should we cling to the ways we've previously "heard" His voice. It's as if we have a "God radio" that we stubbornly keep tuned to our favorite channel. Though there are thousands of spiritual signals that we could choose, we only "listen" to heaven on a very small bandwidth. In the realm of available sound, we often keep ourselves tuned to one frequency.

Therefore, we must accept the reality that God is a talking God who utilizes every nuance of sound to communicate to His creation. So if He is indeed a prolific talker, then He is a God of sound, noise, and language; He is a God that created something from nothing by the vibration of His voice. Actually, God so loves the sound of language that He refers to

Himself in the Bible as the "Living Word." Perhaps that is why the book of Revelation describes no more than 30 minutes of silence in heaven.

Being that God is a talking God, He is communicating to us non-stop, with unrelenting enthusiasm. Again, the reason we do not perceive the full expression of His Person is that He reveals Himself on wavelengths we have not learned to recognize and receive. That's why I have abandoned the age old question, "Why isn't God talking to me?" I've concluded that such a proficient communicator as God is "speaking" in a million ways, His voice filling every atom in the universe. My concern is not that God remains silent, but rather that He's talking to us on so many levels that we do not know how to interpret the spiritual bandwidths through which He communicates.

Also, I am not discouraged by the fact that our minds are unable to pick up all the frequencies through which God communicates with us. I am aware that our inner-man is often engaged with the spirit realm in simple ways we do not recognize. Many times, what we label as just an "inspired thought," "feeling a witness," or having a "gut feeling" is often a God-vibration, a sound of heaven that comes in simple and natural ways. The same holds true for other human responses to the Spirit, which are too numerous to mention.

Tuning in to God's Bandwidth

So the question before us is, "How do we stretch ourselves beyond our familiar, limited bandwidth of hearing from God?" One of the first things we must do is tune into the spirit realm

Spiritual Synesthesia

with all of our senses and reach out for more of God's Spirit in every way we can. As mentioned previously, because our spirits have been programmed to our favorite spiritual channel, we are preconditioned to stick with what is familiar and comfortable. We haven't fully realized that Creation is a perfect sounding board for the voice of a talking God.

My concern is not that God remains silent, but rather that He's talking to us on so many levels that we do not know how to interpret the spiritual bandwidths through which He communicates.

To illustrate, everything in Creation communicates—animals, rocks, trees, the wind, etc. Even such things as colors, smells, and feelings, can declare the personality and intent of God's heart. On earth, for instance, we have a rainbow of colors that come in seven visible primary colors. However, people who have gone to heaven report that they've seen a broad spectrum of colors that does not exist in the physical world. It's like the colors in heaven exist on a different "wavelength" than the colors on earth. In fact, many who have been to heaven have reported that colors there are alive; they talk, they breathe, they speak. Therefore, only "heavenly eyes" can see and hear them.

Several years ago, I had been sick for a long time. One night, a pulsating blue color came into my room and seemed to be talking to me, trying to communicate a message from

Spiritual Synesthesia

God. Since I did not understand synesthesia at that time, I automatically assumed the message the color was sending was "prophetic information," because typically that's the color many prophetic people associate with spiritual revelation. Now I know so much more. Looking back I realize that the visitation was not merely a prophetic revelation, but was a healing visitation sent to me in living color that caused my health to improve dramatically.

So, heavenly sounds can be more than just something you hear. If the essence of everything is vibrational, then it is fair to say that everything carries its own sound. Actually, there are many different things in the sound and light realm that we have yet to understand. Interestingly, there is a quantum physics debate regarding whether or not our thoughts actually emit a vibration that affects the physical realm around us. If this is the case, we must explore the concept of everything being vibrational. If sound is one of the basic building blocks of everything that exists, then to ignore its ramifications would be totally out of tune with reality.

To conclude with the first part of my question, I want to restate several key points. Clearly, one of the greatest revivals in human history–the vibration of heaven in Acts—set all kinds of things in motion. Why? Because, the 120 believers in the Upper Room didn't get hung up on sound alone. They let the sound take them somewhere else, triggering all their senses to the point that they were drunk from the vibration. Also, they had an expectation that was bigger than their ability to understand the Spirit realm. They were waiting for something new, something fresh, and they were not disappointed. A wind from heaven came, and the rest, as they say, is history.

Now to answer the second part of the question about the ways we can stretch ourselves to receive from God. Perhaps the most significant thing we can do to position ourselves for the "new sound" is to start recovering the truths that are currently held captive by many unbelievers. Many New Agers, for example, have already begun to explore the phenomenon of synesthesia and are desperately trying to "tune in" to multiple realms of spiritual reality. In a small measure, many have succeeded in this spiritual quest.

So, what does this mean for us? I believe that much of the spiritual discoveries of the New Age movement could be likened to the time in the Old Testament when the Philistines stole the Ark of the Covenant from Israel. In both cases, then and now, that which belongs to the church fell into the hands of unbelievers. So, in order to posture ourselves for the next move of God, like King David, we must take back what is ours. Certain dynamics such as synesthesia, quantum physics, and "vibrations" are God-stuff, and we must not be afraid to seize what belongs to the Creator of all things.

However, I suspect that many have a fear of being deceived by things they might not understand. Like Israel in the Old Testament, they are quick to relinquish anything that appears different or "spooky" in the spirit realm to the hands of the Philistines. In which case, we need the spirit of David to rise up within us and declare, "I'm taking back what belongs to God!" Furthermore, when we do recover the ark, we must not treat it lightly. We must remember that David offered many sacrifices, sang, danced, and then repeated the process until he got the ark back where it belonged—in the House of God.

Finally, it shouldn't be a surprise that David was a worshiping musician. It was his worshiping spirit that played a big part in taking back the Ark. This says to me that the coming sound of worship and warfare is going to be much more than we've previously imagined. Because we are currently experiencing so little of the sound of heaven, we need people who understand what David understood about taking back the ark.

The Sound of His Voice

Recently, the Lord has been speaking to me about the many ways He reveals Himself. One of the ways is the sound of silence. Heartfelt silence, in fact, is one of the most powerful forms of worship that can leave a person awestruck with God's glory. When our hearts are in tune with inner-silence before the Creator, every aspect of our body quietly speaks. Our cells, minds, and hearts all talk—as they cry out to God without intelligible words.

Actually, every part of our being has a spiritual bandwidth, a "new song," if you will. So, playing instruments and singing is but a small part of what worship can be. Our whole being can make a distinct sound to which God will respond.

When a baby cries, for example, the parent will run to the sound of that voice. The child may not make an intelligent sound, but the parent is sensitive to the sound of the baby. The same is true of our Father God. When we sincerely groan or yell for help, He will respond. Also, when we become totally still, our silence speaks loudly to God. Both are important to turning on a spiritual frequency that attracts our Heavenly Father.

Throughout my life I have experienced several encounters of this nature. At 24, I was caught up into the spirit realm where I saw God seated on His throne. Immediately, I noticed that the heavens and earth were ready to flee from His face, because they were not able to behold His glory. He then turned to look at me, and as He did, it seemed like the whole galaxy turned in synchronization with the movement of His head. When He finally did look at me, I heard the cells in my body scream in unison, "Hide me, from the face of Him who sits on the throne!" I then realized that my body was telling me that if I entertained any more than the briefest of glances from God, I would surely die.

After this experience I felt drunk for several days. I was so impacted by the encounter that my insides were shaking in awe and my body was so weak that I could barely walk. It was like I had a chiropractic adjustment of my spirit—or I could say that I had a vibrational adjustment. Either way, I was left with the reality that every part of our being "communicates" and can receive from God. Even the smallest cell can recognize the Person of God and respond.

Several decades after that encounter I felt compelled to write the book *Spirit Talk*. However, at the time it seemed to be a premature concept that God would speak in colors, numbers, smell, intuition, etc. Now it seems that people are beginning to open their hearts to the many ways that God

Spiritual Synesthesia

communicates to us. As for the subject of synesthesia, what if God chooses to speak more frequently in colors and numbers in this next outpouring? What if he uses colors, numbers, smell, feeling, and sound at the same time? Or speaks to us in a combination of modalities that are physical, mental, and emotional, or even vibrational? Are we really open to "new things" in God?

The answer should be yes! And our cry should be, "Speak to us God! We are now aware that You want to activate our spiritual and physical eyes, ears, taste, smell, and other senses. No longer will we allow our minds to block out the sound of heaven because of our religious dogma. We are committed to developing the sensitivity of our spirit, soul, and body, so that we can experience all the different ways Heaven expresses itself."

So, come Breath of God and sweep us away into a new dimension of Pentecost.

The preceding chapter was adapted from an interview with Larry Randolph.

We'd love to hear about any experiences you might have had with "spiritual synesthesia." Go to www.heavensphysics.com/chapter10 or scan this QR code on your smartphone to share your experiences.

Synesthesia

Imagine that when you see a cat, you taste oranges. Or maybe when you hear people arguing, you see fireworks. Perhaps you are completely convinced that the number 3 tastes salty and is female. If you have experiences like these, you might have synesthesia.

Synesthesia is a condition in which one sense, for example, hearing, is simultaneously perceived as if by one or more additional senses, such as sight, taste, or smell. The word synesthesia comes from two Greek words, syn (together) and aisthesis (perception). Synesthesia literally means "joined perception."

Synesthesia affects approximately 4% of the population. It is also commonly experienced by those who meditate and has been reported by individuals under the influence of psychedelic drugs, after a stroke, or as a result of blindness or deafness. Synesthesia also occurs with autism and epilepsy more often than chance predicts.

The most common effects are grapheme-color (associating a color with letters or numbers) and sound-color. The least common are sound-odor, temperature-color, taste-touch, touch-smell, vision-touch, colored pain and colored personalities. Any combination of the senses is possible.

Music and Near-Death Experiences

Most of us have heard accounts of people seeing bright light during a near-death experience. But according to Dr. Joel Funk, a professor of psychology at Plymouth State College in New Hampshire, nearly 50% of near-death experiencers also report hearing music. Dr. Funk played various kinds of music for 60 near-death experiencers and found that they identified New Age synthesized music as nearest to what they had heard.

Not only do people who have a near-death experience hear music, but they also report that everything is alive and singing. They say that trees, plants, and flowers sing, colors can be heard and sound is on a level beyond hearing but actually vibrates inside their heads and bodies. They also report seeing geometric patterns and colors that don't exist in this realm.

Here are some of their descriptions of NDE music: transcendental, unearthly harmonic beauty, sublimely beautiful, a celestial choir of angels, joyous and beat-less melody, an orchestra of voices, the Music of the Spheres, mystical tones, music that transcends all thought, bells and wind chimes, and music that is experienced from within.

11

Strange Things Are Afoot
by Ellyn Davis

Remember Sir Isaac Newton who supposedly was sitting under a tree when an apple fell on his head and he had his "aha" moment about gravity? He went on to create the framework of physics laws that explain gravity, movement, work systems, heat, sound, light, electricity and magnetism. Newtonian physics has put men on the moon, planes in the air, cars on the roads, skyscrapers in our cities, and computers in our homes.

Newtonian physics views the world as a machine that you can learn about by studying how its different parts interact. It assumes that we are separate from the machine, so we may tinker with it all we want, but merely observing it will have no influence on how it runs.

Think of it this way. Newtonian physics assumes the world is like a big clock that runs on its own. Although I can learn a lot about how the clock works by taking it apart and studying its gears, springs, and dials, me looking to see what time it is will never affect how the clock ticks. In other words, if it's 2 o'clock in the morning, unless I change the dials or a miracle occurs, my watch will never say 10 PM just because I want it to.

Strange Things Are Afoot

The Mystery of Light

Everyone was perfectly happy with the Newtonian explanation of how the world worked until 1900 when Max Planck made a startling discovery about light. Until that time, it was possible to describe all known physical phenomena as either particles or waves.

Physicists already knew that light acted like a wave—like a sound wave or a radio wave—not like solid matter. But Planck proved that light was made up of packets of energy that were like minute particles. The mystery of how light could be both a wave and a particle lead to the discovery that all nature is made up of indivisible units or packets of energy that were later collectively called "quanta". Interest in learning exactly what these quanta were and how they behaved led to the birth of a new branch of physics—quantum physics.

Through quantum physics, scientists have discovered that, at the most basic level of existence, everything is constantly vibrating energy and that every particle also possesses a wave character and every wave possesses a particle character.

But the fact that particles could become waves and waves become particles wasn't the only shock. What was even more shocking was that at the quantum level the world no longer acted like a machine but seemed to act more like something alive that senses the desire of the observer and responds to it.

This meant, if I had a "quantum" clock, it just might tell me the time based on the time I expect it to be. So if I want it to be 10 PM, there would be a probability that when I looked at my quantum watch, it will tell me that it's 10 PM just because that's the time I expect it to be.

Strange Things are Afoot in Quantum Physics

There is a line in the movie *Bill and Ted's Excellent Adventure* that I absolutely love. When confronted with the prospect of a time-traveling phone booth in their Circle K parking lot, Ted turns to Bill and says, "Bill, strange things are afoot at the Circle K."

The same thing could be said of quantum physics. Strange things are afoot! Physicists studying the quantum realm seem baffled by it and consistently use words like "shock," "mystery," and "weird" when explaining their findings.

Neils Bohr, one of the founders of quantum physics, remarked, "Those who are not shocked when they first come across quantum theory cannot possibly have understood it" and Bohr's associate Werner Heisenberg expressed his disbelief by asking, "Can nature possibly be so absurd as it seemed to us in these atomic experiments?"

Another of Bohr's associates, John Wheeler remarked, "If you are not completely confused by quantum mechanics, you do not understand it."

Quantum physics theories seem more like science fiction than science fact, but they have been proven repeatedly in many different experiments by many different physicists and have been spectacularly successful at predicting the behavior of all sorts of sub-atomic systems.

Strange Things Are Afoot

Here are just a few of the mind-boggling discoveries of quantum physics:

- Everything that exists is, in its essence, energy.[1]
- Everything, even solid matter like a chair or a tree, vibrates with an invisible field of energy and those vibrations assume a certain frequency depending on the source of the vibration. The vibrational frequency of a tree is different from the frequency of a rock, and different from the frequency of a lizard, and so forth. The only reason this book seems solid to you is that its energy packets are arranged in such a way and vibrating at a specific frequency for you to be able to see it and feel it as solid matter.[2]
- Whether energy expresses itself as a wave or a particle seems to be related to the expectation of the observer. In quantum physics experiments, if the observer is expecting to see waves, the energy behaves as waves, if the observer is expecting to see particles, the energy behaves as particles.[3]
- When they are not being observed or measured, particles of light act as waves. They have no precise location, but exist as "probability fields". But, if they are being observed or measured, they become particles. When observed or measured, the probability field "collapses" the wave into a solid object in a specific place and time. (This is sometimes called "collapsing the quantum wave function" or "popping the qwiff.")
- The same quantum particle can be in more than one place at one time.[4]
- Two sub-atomic particles that have interacted in the past remain connected so that what is done to one instan-

taneously affects the other no matter how far apart the particles are.[5]

- Nothing can be predicted with absolute certainty, but only as probabilities.[6]
- Particles/waves can pop in and out of different dimensions. When not observed, they are in no particular place.[7]
- Quantum particles can instantly move from one location to another faster than the speed of light. In fact, Chinese physicists have documented quantum particles instantaneously traveling over distances up to 10 meters (over 30 feet).[8]
- Time is not linear as in past, present and future. The past, the present and the future are inextricably linked and time seems to be subjective to the observer. What this means is that quantum particles can travel outside of what we think of as time and space.[9]

The Rise of Quantum Mysticism

Because of the great deal of "strangeness afoot" in quantum physics, it has inevitably attracted metaphysical interpretation. Most of that interpretation has leaned towards using quantum physics to reinforce Eastern mystical beliefs about the nature of the oneness of all reality and the power of human consciousness to create and manipulate that reality.

In his book, *Science and the New Age Challenge*, Ernest Lucas traces three key concepts of quantum mysticism. **The first major concept is that the world we live in is not the "real" world, but an illusion.** A corollary to this concept is that, because of our childhood imprinting and societal programming, we don't see the world as it really is.

The second major quantum mysticism concept is that the universe is a unified, inter-connected whole. This translates to the idea that, since all is one, then all must be God which means that you are God and your consciousness is an aspect of the divine consciousness.

Because of the great deal of "strangeness afoot" in quantum physics, it has inevitably attracted metaphysical interpretation. And most of that interpretation has leaned towards using quantum physics to reinforce Eastern mystical beliefs about the nature of the oneness of all reality and the power of human consciousness to manipulate that reality.

The third key concept is the idea that, since material reality needs an observer to make it assume material form, human consciousness, acting as individualized expressions of divine consciousness, has the power to create material reality. Several early quantum physicists were inspired by mystical ideas, including Niels Bohr, Wolfgang Pauli (who worked with Carl Jung on the theory of synchronicity) and Erwin Schrödinger.

Later, quantum mysticism became a part of mainstream thought when Deepak Chopra's 1988 book *Quantum Heal-*

ing used quantum concepts to propose his theory of psychosomatic healing. In 1993, Chopra's New York Times Bestseller *Ageless Body, Timeless Mind* claimed that healing and reversal of aging could be accomplished by adopting a "quantum worldview."

The latest and perhaps most well known theoretical physicist to embrace a mystical interpretation is Dr. Fred Alan Wolf. His appearance in the 2004 film *What the #$*! Do We Know!?* lent scientific credibility to the New Age philosophies presented in the film and popularized the term "popping a qwiff."

What the #$!* became a grass roots phenomenon and was based on teachings supposedly channeled from Ramtha, the 35,000 year old spirit of a warrior from the lost continent of Lemuria. Two years later, in 2006, Wolf appeared in *The Secret*, a film introducing The Law of Attraction, a concept extrapolated from quantum physics that the "observer" can create material reality through intent. *The Secret* was based on New Thought teachings from the early 1900's and, like *What the #$*!,* was influenced by channeled messages from disembodied entities.

If there were anything similar to a New Age Bible, it would be *A Course in Miracles*, a self-study curriculum which aims at helping its readers achieve spiritual transformation through embracing mystical interpretations of quantum physics. Helen Schucman wrote the book based on what she called an "inner voice" she identified as Jesus. Over two million copies of *A Course in Miracles* have been distributed worldwide since it first became available for sale in 1976.

Modern culture is presently awash with metaphysical interpretations of quantum physics such as the The Law of Attraction (the belief that everything has its own vibrational level and like attracts like so to attract what you want you must change your vibrational level to match it), The Law of Intent (the belief that our intent can change physical reality or make material things manifest from the realm of the unseen) and The Law of Thought Vibration (your thoughts and emotions have either positive or negative vibrations and will cause manifestations in your life of things and experiences with similar vibrations).

As Phil Mason explains in his book *Quantum Glory*,

These key concepts, (1) that the material world is really a field of cosmic energy that can be manipulated by consciousness, (2) that we are all a part of a cosmically interconnected whole and (3) that our consciousness is an untapped resource that can shape reality, have emerged into a cluster of powerful ideas that have gripped the popular imagination in the Western world.

However, many quantum concepts appropriated by the New Age are actually distortions of Christian spiritual truths as you will discover in the following chapters.

Notes:
[1]Quantum Physics Principle
- Max Planck, 1918: all of nature is made up of invisible quanta of energy—the smallest units into which

something can be partitioned. The atom is made up of quantum ingredients; therefore the entire universe is made up of quanta (or quantities) of energy.

[2]Quantum Physics Principles:
- Louis de Broglie: "wave-particle duality"—on the atomic and subatomic level both energy and matter behave as if they are made of either particles or waves, depending on their environment, and can seem to materialize and dematerialize from solid matter to vibrations of invisible field energy.
- String theorists: the smallest constituent elements of energy/matter are tiny loops of oscillating, vibrating energy.

[3]Quantum Physics Principles:
- Louis de Broglie, 1927: "Pilot Wave Theory"—each quantum particle has an associated wave function that travels ahead of the particle and detects whether it will be observed or not.
- David Bohm: the Pilot Wave is non-local and therefore not bound by the constraints of time and space.
- "The Observer Effect"—Quantum objects can exist either as waves or particles. Wave functions are collapsed when viewed by an observer and become particles. An object is a cloud of ambiguous possibilities and exists in all possible states simultaneously but assumes a certain state depending on the intent of the observer whether or not it is being observed in the present or the future. Even the smallest quantum object seems to have a "mind" that directs its course

depending on the mind of the observer.

[4]Quantum Physics Principle:
- "Non-locality"—sub-atomic particles have the capacity to be in two places at the same time.

[5]Quantum Physics Principle:
- "Quantum Entanglement"—entangled pairs of photons that have interacted in the past and then moved far away from each other remain, in a certain sense, still connected and what is done to one will affect the other instantaneously.

[6]Quantum Physics Principles:
- Werner Heisenberg: the Heisenberg Uncertainty Principle—features of the universe, like the position and velocity of a particle, cannot be known with complete precision but only as possibilities.
- "Schrödinger's Cat"—quantum indeterminacy, the principle of the "superposition" of the Heisenberg Uncertainty Principle. Put a cat in a sealed box with a vial of cyanide, once it is sealed it is impossible to know with certainty whether the cat is dead or alive and because we cannot have certainty, the cat could be considered both dead and alive.

[7]Quantum Physics Principle:
- "Quantum Tunneling"—matter in the subatomic world has the capacity to de-materialize at one side of a barrier and to re-materialize on the other side.

8. Quantum Physics Principle:
- "Quantum Teleportation"—dematerializing an object at one point and transferring the precise details of its

configuration to another location where the object is then reconstructed.

[9]Quantum Physics Principle:
- "Delayed Choice Experiments"—The whole universe seems to "know" in advance what experiment an individual human being is going to carry out. The quality of time is linked to specific experimental choices and the past is inextricably tied to the present. Time is a product of the observer rather than an objective attribute of space. The flow of time is subjective, not objective. If a quantum particle can "know" the future before it occurs and, similarly, if an act in the present can erase the past it is evident that we are not dealing with a linear arrow of time in our developing understanding of the non-local dimension of quantum space.

Go to www.heavensphysics.com/chapter11 or scan this QR code on your smartphone to share your insights and spiritual experiences about topics covered in this chapter.

The Solfeggio Frequencies

Gregorian chants were based on the Solfeggio frequencies, special tones believed to have transformative power and impart spiritual blessings.

These Solfeggio frequencies use an ancient musical scale of six tones Ut, Re, Mi, Fa, Sol and La. The tone of Ut vibrates at a frequency of 396 Hz, which correlates to a frequency some scientists believe puts a person in the most receptive state to external input. The tone of Mi has a frequency of 528 Hz which many believe strengthens the heart's electromagnetic field.

Some modern-day geneticists believe that, when sung in sequential harmony, the sounds of the musical tones in the Solfeggio scale vibrate at the exact frequencies required to open our cells so new programming can be imprinted on our DNA. Genetic biochemists are already using the frequency of 528 Hz to repair DNA that has been damaged.

In 2010, physicist John Hutchison created a device that emits a combination of audio and radio frequencies based on the Solfeggio frequencies which have the effect of clearing water pollution. Using these vibrational frequencies, Hutchison's device cleared a one mile radius of polluted water in Perdido Bay in the Gulf of Mexico within 24 hours.

12

Quantum Mysticism
by Ellyn Davis

If we stop for a moment and really consider the implications of quantum physics, we can understand how it lends itself to metaphysical interpretation. So let's discuss a few of the main metaphysical beliefs extrapolated from quantum physics and how they might relate to Christian truths.

Metaphysical Interpretations of Quantum Physics

According to Wikipedia, quantum mysticism is the "set of metaphysical beliefs and associated practices that seek to relate consciousness, intelligence or mystical world-views to the ideas of quantum mechanics and its interpretations." Quantum mysticism centers around four main beliefs.

First, there is the belief in the power of consciousness to influence material reality.

In their book *Quantum Enigma*, Bruce Rosenblum and Fred Kuttner explain the mysticism inherent in quantum physics this way:

Quantum Mysticism

Physics has an embarrassing problem. It affects to be a rigorous, hard-headed science, yet quantum mechanics, its most successful theory (it has never made a wrong prediction), seems to rub up inevitably against the problem of consciousness, and even quasi-mystical interpretations of the universe. Why? Because of the extremely odd fact that you can choose to demonstrate either of two contradictory possibilities simply by deciding which experiment to perform. And it is not just "observer-dependent" in a weak sense; by observing a photon, you cause the photon to be there and nowhere else. Before you observed it, it wasn't just in some specific location of which you were ignorant, it was in no particular place at all, or in many places at once.

It seems inconceivable that quantum particles exist as waves in no definite place or time but when observed and measured the wave becomes a solid object in a specific place and time. As already stated, this phenomenon is called "collapsing the quantum wave function" or "popping a qwiff." The fact that it happens forces us to consider two ideas: first that everything is, in its essence, an interconnected invisible field of energies vibrating at different specific frequencies and second, that in order for a particular energy to assume material form, it needs an observer, a "consciousness" expecting it to become matter.

Another idea that "popping a qwiff" forces us to at least entertain is that somehow human consciousness is a fundamental creative force in the Universe, since it is our consciousness (as the "observer") that seems to determine whether something appears as matter or not. If this is true, it means that we have the power to create, manipulate and change the "reality" of our world by our expectations or intentions.

Second, there is the belief in a single, universal consciousness that permeates all things.
The traditional view about consciousness has always been that it is a property of the mind and that consciousness is only shared by beings with brains. Also, it has been understood that conscious beings have differing levels of self-awareness. For example, a human being may be aware that he or she is conscious while a dog may not.

Newtonian physics never considered the possibility that lower life forms, plants, or what we consider inanimate objects such as rocks and stars might have some sort of consciousness too. Quantum physics does.

Quantum physics implies that everything that exists, even atoms and sub-atomic particles, has a form of consciousness (sometimes called a "mind") and is interconnected through a universal consciousness (the One Mind). This would explain "quantum entanglement" effects, also called "spooky action at a distance" by Einstein.

In quantum entanglement a particle that has been "entangled" with another particle "knows" whether to assume the property of a wave or a particle according to what has happened to the other particle no matter if that particle is across the room or on Jupiter. That information is mysteriously transferred instantaneously at speeds beyond the speed of light.

A view of one interconnected consciousness in all things would explain this mystery because it would mean that one particle would be receiving its information on what was happening to the other particle from a non-local level of reality. This "one consciousness" idea would also explain many behaviors that have baffled scientists such as how a flock of birds or a school of fish can all turn instantaneously without colliding as if the group shares a common mind.

Scientists have studied this phenomenon for decades but have found no completely satisfactory answer to the mystery of why a wave of movement can radiate through a flock of birds or school of fish almost three times faster than is possible according to the animal's visual or auditory reaction times.

Even humans are capable of this behavior. It is dubbed the "chorus line effect." Films of human chorus lines show that maneuvers such as a high leg kick, initiated without warning at one end of the line, will move down the rest of the line almost twice as fast as should be possible according to human visual reaction time.

Another human example of "interconnected as through a common consciousness" behavior is synchronized clapping. An applauding audience can usually synchronize its clapping in less than two beats.

Third, there is the belief that everything—even our thoughts and emotions—emits energetic vibrations.
Quantum Physics suggests that everything is "vibrations"—

fields of vibrating energy. However, quantum mysticism claims that even our thoughts and emotions give off vibrations or energies. Many people believe this without attributing it to quantum physics because we've all had experiences such as sensing the tension when we walk into a room where people have been arguing. Metaphysicists would say we are picking up the "vibrations" of anger.

There is also the belief that some vibrations are good for us and give off healing energy while some vibrations give off damaging, unhealthy energy. States of higher consciousness are states of higher, more positive energy while lower states of consciousness are due to negative energies.

Therefore, most metaphysical, New Age, and oriental healing modalities center around techniques for ridding ourselves of negative energies and balancing our flow of positive energy in order to reach states of better health and higher consciousness.

Fourth, there is the belief in parallel universes.

Quantum theories about parallel universes, other dimensions, and a "multiverse" cause us to wonder if there is another side to reality and it is that "other side" that is the origin of our consciousness and the real cause of everything that happens on "this side." Hans-Peter Dürr, former director of the renowned Max Planck Institute for physics in Munich, said this about the "other side" of reality:

> *What we call the material world is the slag, matter, everything that can be touched. The "other side" is everything else, the greater reality, the much bigger side of reality.*

Quantum Mysticism

The one consciousness and "other side" theories also provide an explanation for the mystery of what happens when our body dies. If we assume that our actual origin is the "other side," an essential part of us (commonly referred to as our soul) continues to exist through quantum entanglement.

Not only that, but our consciousness can continue to process and store information even after our physical death. This idea is corroborated by many reports of near-death or out-of-body experiences—even those that occurred when there was no brain activity. People who have actually died and come back to life have been able to accurately describe all that was going on around them immediately after their death.

But since the nature of this "other side" where the soul originates is non-local, it must also mean that all souls are non-locally connected; all souls are somehow connected to one field of consciousness, one "universal mind."

And it is not just our souls that are connected, but everything in the universe is interconnected through the field of infinite consciousness—people, birds, plants, rocks, trees, clouds, stars. This means that the true nature of the universe is oneness, not duality (like in Newtonian physics where the "observer" was separate from "the observed").

Fifth, there is the belief that mankind is evolving to higher levels of consciousness.
Quantum mysticism teaches that as we begin to more fully understand and experience the implications of the oneness of all things, we will take an evolutionary leap of consciousness. At this higher level of consciousness, our experiences

of being one with all that is will actually become a way of life, and we will consistently be able to alter the nature of reality with our thoughts and intentions. This is the traditional view of what happens in enlightenment.

Compatibilities with Christianity?

It's obvious that the New Age has used quantum physics as part of its belief structure. But are any of the ideas advanced by quantum mysticism compatible with Christianity?

Yes, they are. I think the beliefs of quantum mysticism are compatible with Christianity in many ways but are totally incompatible in a few, most important ways.

Christians and quantum mystics part ways over four issues: (1) where God, Jesus, and the Holy Spirit fit into the picture; (2) what constitutes sin; (3) where the Bible fits into the picture: and (4) what happens after we die. I won't go into these incompatabilities here, but you may read them on the website *www.heavensphysics.com*.

However, there is much that we can agree on. In fact, as the authors of some chapters in this book have mentioned, all truth is God's truth and there are many precious "God-truths" hidden in Quantum Mysticism for us to claim as our own. We'll delve into just a few of them in the rest of this chapter.

God-Truth: By Faith, We Can Speak Things Into Existence

Christians believe that through faith (which could be considered a form of "intent") we can affect changes in the material world, and, as Romans 4: 17 says, "call the things that are not as if they are." We also know that words and the intent behind them have such incredible power that the Bible tells us, "life and death are in the power of the tongue."

In the natural realm, words can hurt or heal and in the spiritual realm words can carry God's power and authority and bring the promises of God's Word from the unseen spiritual world into the natural. After all, our faith is "the substance of things hoped for, the evidence of things unseen" and Jesus told us that if we have even the smallest amount of faith, we can speak out what we want and have it happen ("if you have faith as a mustard seed, you can say to this mountain, be removed" Matthew 17: 20).

It shouldn't be a stretch for us to believe that, as "observers" to whom Jesus gave all power in heaven and earth, we can, through faith, intent, prayer and declaration, call things into existence. Jesus has given us the power, through our faith and our intent, to "pop a qwiff" and bring things from the unseen world into the visible.

Modern day scientific examples of the power of faith, intent, prayer, and declaration are found in the studies of prayer researcher Jack Stucki. Stucki measured the electrical activity in both the brain and body surface of his test subjects and found the readings could be altered if the subjects were prayed for by groups as far as 1,000 miles away.

God-Truth: Thoughts and Attitudes Are Powerful

Since Christians believe that our thoughts and attitudes ("the thoughts and intents of the heart") can have a powerful influence on the world around us, it shouldn't be hard for us to accept that thoughts and emotions might actually give off energetic "vibrations" that can cause changes in the physical and emotional atmosphere.

In fact, Dr. Walter Weston reports in *Prayer Heals* that most people emit a variable electromagnetic frequency from their hands but healers emit a steady 7.8 hertz frequency that approximates the Schumann Resonance, the earth's resonant frequency. Researchers have also shown that the hands of spiritual healers can emit over 200 volts of electricity whereas non-healers' hands produce no more than 4 volts. 200 volts is more than the voltage used in electrocardioversion to reset heart rhythm.

Many healers also believe that strong emotions are stored in energy fields in the heart as well as in other cells of our bodies. Neuropsychologist Dr. Paul Pearsall, clinical professor at the University of Hawai'i observed that many heart transplant recipients assume the donor's tastes, behavior, preferences, sexual desires and vocabulary and sometimes even their memories. Dr. Alexander Lloyd, author of *The Healing Code* teaches that the negative energies trapped in our cells by trauma and stress are the cause of many of our emotional and physical ailments.

It shouldn't be hard for us to believe that the "vibrational energy" we emit in the world can attract thoughts, emotions, and experiences that are in harmony with ours.

For example, have you ever noticed that when you are in a really good mood you can walk into a store and everyone seems to be smiling at you but when you wake up on the wrong side of the bed your day tends to go downhill from there?

Christians also should have no trouble believing that some vibrations are good for us and give off healing energies while some vibrations give off damaging, unhealthy energies.

After all, we believe in demonic forces that seek to kill, steal and destroy and angelic forces that seek to help us in our walk with God, so it should be easy for us to believe that some states of consciousness are states of positive energy while others are due to negative energies.

In fact, some Christian leaders believe that spirit beings such as demons and angels exist on different "bandwidths" or frequencies than human beings and that is why we seldom see them or are aware of the ways they are affecting our lives.

God-Truth: A Oneness Connection?

We already believe that during the creation of the universe God caused energy to transform into matter and He has continued to work creative miracles through the power of His Holy Spirit. So, in effect, God could be thought of as the "ultimate observer."

Scripture tells us that rocks can cry out, stars can sing, and trees can "clap their hands" in joy, so we wouldn't be too surprised to discover that they have a form of consciousness too, a "mind" as it were.

We also know that we all share some mystical connection with each other, with all things, and with ultimate consciousness because we've had unexplainable experiences of connectivity like feeling someone else's pain or thinking of an old friend we haven't seen for years and suddenly running into them at a restaurant. If there weren't some universal connectedness, why would God treat us as "all in Adam" or "all in Christ?" And why could Paul say that all of creation "groans and waits" for us to assume our full manifestation as sons and daughters of God?

God-Truth: Different Levels of Reality?

We already know that there are vast unseen realms populated with beings of varying degrees of consciousness and power and that the "real" dimension of ultimate reality isn't on this earth. The Bible speaks of different "levels" of spiritual habitation (the third heaven, for example) which could all be different dimensions of reality. So we should have no problem embracing theories about the "other side" and multiple dimensions of reality.

In addition, we believe that the closer and more dedicated our walk with God is, the more we can fully understand and experience the implications of what it means to be "one" with Him like Jesus was. We also believe that our experiences of being one with Him can actually become a way of life to the point that we will consistently be able to alter the nature of reality with our words, thoughts and intentions.

Go to www.heavensphysics.com/chapter12 or scan this QR code on your smartphone to share your insights and spiritual experiences on topics covered in this chapter.

The Power of Color

In the 17th century, Isaac Newton observed that when a narrow beam of sunlight passes through a glass prism, the light emerges as a rainbow of different colored bands. Newton divided the spectrum of colors into seven: red, orange, yellow, green, blue, indigo, and violet. He chose seven colors out of a belief derived from the Greeks that there was a connection between the colors, musical notes, known objects in the solar system, and the days of the week. This range of colors is called the visible bandwidth because it contains the only wavelengths of electromagnetic light the human eye can discern.

Since Newton's time, light and color have been shown to affect humans physically and psychologically. For example, studies show that the color pink temporarily calms aggression, so some holding cells for violent criminals are painted pink. Green has also been shown to have a calming effect so is often used in psychiatric hospitals. Red increases concentration abilities and blue enhances creativity. Some scientists believe that your skin as well as your eyes can perceive the frequencies of different colors.

13

Keys to Taking Your Quantum Leap
by David Van Koevering

In this chapter, David Van Koevering explains that, because of the laws of quantum physics, our spoken intent can bring something from the unseen realm into the seen and we can make the non-material appear in material form. In other words, we can "pop qwiffs." There is a non-physical reality from which this universe and everything in it flows. Jesus Himself is causing your body, your spirit, and everything you have to blink into your reality. All the things of life and their purpose for you and your assignment are frequencies being spoken by Christ Himself at this very nanosecond.

Years ago, as a young scientist and inventor, I worked with Dr. Bob Moog and together we gave the music world the first performance keyboards called Moog synthesizers. I learned to work with electrons and photons—tiny elements that are so small they can't be seen! Yet these invisible elements cause all electronic devices to work. This project caused me to ask the question, "Is there more to our universe than what I can perceive through my senses?"

My search to learn more about physical reality and how it works led me to discover that quantum physics identifies a large part of our universe to be non-physical.

I began to realize that the universe is greater than science has discovered or can explain. Through quantum physics and spiritual revelation, the Holy Spirit confirmed keys to understanding physical reality. As you read this chapter, allow the Holy Spirit to let you hear more than I say.

There is a Non-Physical Reality

My studies in quantum mechanics led me to the works of Max Planck, Albert Einstein, Niels Bohr, and others. Here I learned that everything we see is part of a vast ocean of infinitesimally small subatomic particles. Under certain conditions, these subatomic structures also take on the properties of invisible waves.

When I learned that these waves, or particles which make up all matter, cause that matter to blink into existence by being observed by the experimenter, I was shaken to my core.

How could it be that these invisible elements, which make up all matter, can be changed from particles to waves by how they are observed? This reality is beyond our human consciousness and our five senses. Or is it?

All of these particles and/or waves appear to be connected. How can it be that every atomic and subatomic element is hooked up? Is this invisible world a part of the spiritual realm?

I suppose the duality of matter being waves or particles and how quantum mechanics attempts to explain this revolutionary idea changed me forever. It caused me to do my own research, which led to the convergence of quantum mechanics and my personal spiritual revelation. I was about to take a quantum leap!

Is there more to our universe that what I can perceive through my senses?

---

1 Corinthians 1:28 says, "...God (has) chosen...things which are not (the invisible) to bring to naught things which are (the visible)." This Scripture makes sense only when you understand it at the atomic and subatomic level. Everything is made up of atoms, which are frequencies of energy. These frequencies of energy are the voice of Jesus causing all things to be! Atoms are made up of subatomic particles, and subatomic particles are made up of superstrings, tiny donut shaped packets of energy that spin at a specific frequency—or sing as in a pitch.

None of this is real in this dimension because they exist only in a state of possibilities until someone observes them. Then, at that observation, the potential becomes a thing—a particle or a wave. This quantum wave collapse, caused by observation, is your first step to taking a quantum leap. You can see or observe a God qwiff (something God shows you that is not yet real in this dimension) and, by observing, or popping that qwiff, cause that potential to become your reality. Be careful what you see; you are going to get it! Be careful what you say; you will get that, too!

Light is Slowing Down

The spiritual realm operates above the speed of light. The physical realm–this dimension–has been shaped to its current limits by the falls of both Lucifer (see Luke 10:18) and man in the Garden of Eden (see Genesis 3:7). When man fell, the speed of light slowed down. In the beginning, when God spoke the universe into existence, His entire bandwidth of glory was made physical. From His glory (all frequencies) and His voice (all frequencies expressed) all light, energy, and matter became.

It is believed that the speed of light is 186,000 miles per second. Physicist Barry Setterfield and mathematicians Trevor Norman and Alan Montgomery have measured light and proven that the speed of light is slowing down.

That means that light may have been ten to thirty percent faster in the time of Christ; twice as fast in the days of Solomon; and four times as fast in the days of Abraham.

It would also imply that the velocity of light could have been more than ten million times faster prior to 3,000 B.C. This possibility would also alter our concepts of time and the age of the universe. The universe might actually be less than 10,000 years old! That sounds like a quantum leap to me!

It also means there once could have been more bandwidths than contained in this present human realm which contains bandwidths through the electromagnetic spectrum to the speed of light. The interesting point about the speed of light slowing down is that when Lucifer (the bearer of light) rebelled in Heaven and was cursed and cast down—and I believe cast down from the frequencies of God's glory—he lost his bandwidth and fell down from his spiritual consciousness. In the Garden of Eden, when mankind sinned, was cursed in the fall downward, and lost upper bandwidth and spiritual consciousness, light slowed down even more.

Other Biblical events suggest that the cosmos lost bandwidth. Noah's flood is such an example. Light slowed down to cause just the right frequencies for the rainbow (see Genesis 9:12-17). At Nimrod's Tower of Babel, mankind lost the upper bandwidth to communicate (see Genesis 11:7).

Jesus Himself told His disciples that they will get their upper bandwidth back. In John 16:13 He said, "..when He, the Spirit of Truth, is come, He will guide you into all truth... and He will show you things to come." Jesus is saying, "I want to show you your future. You can know My will and My plan for your life, although right now, you don't have the upper bandwidth to see or observe it. But when the Spirit of truth comes, He will give you the upper bandwidth to see things to come!"

Here is a quantum leap for someone: If you know something coming from your future, let's say a vision, a revelation, a desire, or even a creative idea, that information has to move faster than the speed of light to reach you.

You can and must know your God-given assignment. Information flowing from your future possibilities is waiting for you to see—to observe—and call those things that are not as though they are. The quantum leap of knowing your purpose and assignment is waiting as a God qwiff for you to pop!

Matter is Frequency Being Spoken by Jesus

When God spoke and all the frequencies of His glory became manifest, the cosmos became! From the tiniest vibrating superstring that is causing or singing the atoms that make up the table of 118 elements, all the way through everything the Hubble telescope sees, are the vibrating frequencies of Jesus' voice.

Colossians 1:16-17 says, "For by Him all things were created that are in Heaven and that are on earth, visible and invisible... He is before all things, and in Him all things consist (exist or are sustained)." The phrase "He is before all things" means that He is outside of our time. Jesus said to John the Revelator that He was and is the Alpha (beginning) and Omega (ending). Jesus is outside our concept of time. He is in the eternal now and is causing all things to be.

Our false concepts regarding time and matter limit our understanding when we consider creation and all things eternal. Receive the concept that Jesus is outside of our time and calendar, looking in. He is observing. He is sustaining all things in this nanosecond (one billionth of a second) and is singing the frequencies or vibrations of your body. If He didn't, you would dissolve! Your electrons, particles, and subatomic structures are blinking in and out of existence.

You think you are a solid object, but quantum mechanics has confirmed that all subatomic particles—the stuff you are made of—are blinking in and out of this reality.

Enoch was walking so closely with God in the Spirit that "he was not, for God took him" (see Genesis 5:24). Jesus simply stopped blinking Enoch into this realm! How close are you to Jesus Christ? How far away is your healing, your deliverance, or your miracle? He is close, for in Him you live and move and have your being.

In the next nanosecond, He sustains you or sings your frequency set. Understand that your healing or miracle is within the next nanosecond! In the blink of a nanosecond, He can cause your healing. Observe your healing, your miracle, your deliverance, and be filled with all Truth by observing the future God has for you. Take that quantum leap!

Our false concepts regarding time and matter limit our understanding when we consider creation and all things eternal.

When we understand that we are being created in Christ by His causing, or by Him singing our song, our intimacy with Him will change. His song of creation was not something He did billions of years ago. He is causing you now!

Because, through Him, we have our upper bandwidth back, and because He is sustaining us every nanosecond, the act of creation is happening now! Take your quantum leap into His eternal now.

All Matter Has Memory

As a scientist and inventor, I have developed various memory retrieval systems. In the 1970's, I developed a laser optical music system to store sounds on silver oxide film and play the sounds back with keyboards, using modulated light beams.

I was amazed when I found the Scripture in Joshua 24:27 that says, "And Joshua said unto all the people, 'Behold, this stone shall be a witness unto us; for it hath heard all the words of the LORD which He spake unto us: it shall be therefore a witness unto you, lest you deny your God.'"

Was this an Old Testament quantum physicist saying that matter has memory? Is this man, who called for and observed the sun standing still in the heavens, telling us that the stone is listening? This is the man who sounded a frequency that cancelled the frequencies of matter in the walls of Jericho, thereby dissolving their atomic lattice structure with his shout and song. Did this man say the rocks are listening?

Jesus said the same thing. Joshua said the stone could record, and Jesus said in Luke 19:40 that the stones would cry out. Habakkuk 2:11 says, "For the stone shall cry out of the wall, and the beam out of the timber shall answer it." I came to understand that all matter has memory. The Bible says that matter can record and it will play back. How can these things be?

As I studied both quantum theory and Scripture, revelation came. I learned that Gerald Feinberg, a physicist at Columbia University, named a certain subatomic particle that he found in Einstein's math after the Greek word tachys, meaning "swift." He called this superluminal particle a tachyon. This particle moved faster than light!

The tachyon is not looked upon favorably by physicists. If tachyons can be proven to exist and anything that moves faster than light can be found, scientists will have to explain how something can appear before its cause. For instance, if a scientific test were set up to look for this elusive faster-than-light tachyon, and the computer started at 12:00 noon counting forward through the test sequence, the test result wouldn't be at 12:01 or later. It would show the effect before the cause at 11:59 or earlier. Scientists don't have computers that count backwards and don't accept results that appear before the cause.

But wait. Two thirds of your Bible got to mankind before the event or cause! All prophecy is the result of facts before the event. All creativity comes before the actual physical reality!

What is a vision? What is a word of knowledge? It is seeing, knowing, getting information before the causation.

All truth comes to man through the only source of truth we have, and that is the Holy Spirit. There is no other source of creativity than the Holy Spirit. When you see your future, you are getting information faster than the speed of light through a means of streaming superluminal particles. The barrier of light speed is bridged from this subluminal realm to the higher bandwidth of the superluminal realm by the Holy Spirit.

Something like Gerald Feinberg's tachyon exists in all matter. It is just above, or faster than the speed of light. We know it's there because we find the results of such in the very fact of prophecy, or in the concept of words of knowledge, and even our Bible itself. These are proofs that the potential and possibilities of future promises or information is flowing to us. The superluminal tachyon-like connector exists!

Today, it is not difficult to believe that matter has memory, because most of us have tiny memory sticks or memory cards that record or store information from our cameras and computers. Information flowing into matter and recalling it is commonplace. Photons from all light sources reflect from your body and off your belongings. Those information carrying photons go into all matter, including walls, your ring, and your watch. This information—even what we say and think—is modulating or moving through the connectedness of all atomic structures. This modulated photon goes in and electrons come out. That is why Joshua said, "This stone has heard." Every word, action, and deed done in the flesh has been recorded.

This is where yesterday went! It is all recorded in matter and will someday be played back. This is how evil and curses reside in places or things. Even though matter has recorded everything, your prayer in the name of Jesus can take the effect of Christ's blood—His blood that is eternal and beyond time—and cancel out all evil, sin, and past sin's memory from matter. Oh, that is a quantum leap for many! You can speak to and erase from places all curses and evil in Jesus' name.

Have you fixed your past? Have you removed all curses? Have you blessed the things you own? Have you blessed your house, office, car, belongings, money, computer, and phone? Are those things and places free from your past actions, words, and thoughts? You or someone else can speak a blessing or curse on your things. Somebody is about to take a quantum leap!

Keys to Your Quantum Leap

Seeing Your Future as God Sees It

Hebrews 11:1 says that faith is a substance. It is the invisible substance from which your physical world was and is being created by Jesus Christ. Annette Capps said, "God used faith substance and word energy to create the universe. He spoke and the vibration (sound) of His words released (caused) the substance that became the stars and planets."

You can see or observe a God qwiff (something God shows you that is not yet real in this dimension) and, by observing or popping that qwiff, cause that potential to become your reality.

God's future potential and all the promised possibilities constantly flow through the Holy Spirit into you. Noise on my circuit limits my ability to hear His voice and see His future for me. The noise in my inner man is not always sin; my noise can be my gift, my ability, even that special way I am put together and wired. I can become so busy-noisy that I am out of phase with God's voice and vision for me.

As I get quiet and become still, I can hear and see what God's future is for my reality. Psalm 46:10 says, "Be still and know that I am God..." My future comes from God's possibilities and potential. I pop God's qwiffs and my reality is! What an awesome quantum leap!

Keys to Your Quantum Leap

Matter has memory, and you can change everything that has been recorded by what you observe, by the words you declare, or by the curses you remove and release in the name of Jesus. You can create protected places by anointing with oil and speaking blessings with your words of faith.

Where will you start? What quantum leaps have come up in your spirit? You have been given a new cosmic consciousness. Pop those God qwiffs and cause upper bandwidth to change your reality!

This chapter is excerpted from an article by David Van Koevering entitled "Keys to Taking Your Quantum Leap."

Go to www.heavensphysics.com/chapter13 or scan this QR code on your smartphone to share your insights and spiritual experiences on topics covered in this chapter.

Popping Qwiffs by Faith

Annette Capps says that faith is an energy force that affects the vibrational realm and can cause things to be brought from the invisible realm into the visible, "Faith is an unseen energy force. It is not matter, but it creates matter and actually becomes matter. You have a choice to use the energy of your words to change matter."

According to quantum physics, a particular, specific reality does not exist until it is selected and observed. Before being selected, its existence on the physical plane was a reality only in probability.

"Popping a qwiff" is a quantum physics term for the transformation of a wave into a particle by the intent of the observer. In other words, everything exists as energy in a formless, wave-like state with the possibility of becoming a particle of solid matter. Then, by the act of observation, the wave-function is "collapsed" and the selected reality comes into actual existence. All realities only exist in probability until a particular reality is selected. If this is true, it means we can bring into existence whatever reality we have chosen by "popping that qwiff."

Mind Over Matter?

By this point in the book, you've realized that you have a choice to use the energy of your intent and your words to change matter and events. Knowing this, you want to speak faith-energized words to your children, your finances, your health, and your circumstances. But is there any scientific proof that a person's intent actually can affect matter?

Scientists at the Princeton Engineering Anomalies Research lab at Princeton University have demonstrated a connection between intention and the behavior of quantum electronic devices called Random Event Generators.

Their researchers have experimentally explored the effects of human intention on the behavior of random physical systems such as water fountains, pendulums and other devices for more than twenty five years. Results of 840,000 trials per intention by 91 different individuals over a 12 year period showed statistically significant correlations between operator intentions and the output of the random event generators. The likelihood of the results being due to chance alone was less than 5 in 100,000, an extraordinarily high degree of significance.

14

Whole Lotta Shaking Going On

Many men and women of God have experienced physical shaking and "vibrating" and seen bright light when undergoing a deep spiritual transformation. Others have described sensations like electric shocks when encountering God's presence. Here are just a few stories from contributors to this book and others who have had transformative experiences that involved vibrating, electrical sensations, and light.

Bill Johnson

In 1995, I began to cry out to God day and night for around eight months. My prayer was, "God, I want more of you at any cost! I will pay any price!" Then, one night in October, God came in answer to my prayer, yet not in a way I had expected. I went from being in a dead sleep to being wide-awake in a moment. Unexplainable power began to surge through my body. If I had been plugged into a wall socket with a thousand volts of electricity flowing through my body, I can't imagine that it would have been much different. It was as though an extremely powerful being had entered the room and I could not function in His presence. My arms and legs shot out in silent explosions as this power was released through my hands and feet. The more I tried to stop it, the worse it got.

I soon discovered that this was not a wrestling match I was going to win. I heard no voice, nor did I have any visions. This was simply the most overwhelming experience of my life. It was raw power…it was God. He came in response to the prayer I had been praying.

Now, the evening preceding this encounter had been glorious. Our church had been having a series of meetings with a good friend and prophet, Dick Joyce, and had enjoyed an outstanding time of God's presence and power manifested in the lives of His people that night.

During the ministry time, a friend of mine had a hard time receiving from God, and I felt I had a word to give him from God. I told him that God was going to visit him and touch him in a powerful way, and that it could happen at any time of the day or night—perhaps two in the afternoon or even three in the morning. It would come as a surprise.

After the meeting, we finally got to bed around 1:00 a.m. When I was awakened by the power of God, I looked at the clock and saw that it was 3:00 a.m. exactly. I spoke out loud to the Lord, "You set me up!" God had set me up with the prophecy I had given to my friend

Several times throughout the ten years before this I had experienced the same kind of power in the middle of the night, but only in my legs, and much less in intensity. I did not know it was God. I had always thought something was wrong with my body.

Whole Lotta Shaking

I would get out of bed and eat a banana, thinking the potassium might help. When that did not work, I would take an anti-inflammatory drug, thinking that might bring relief. It never helped either.

This time, at 3:00 a.m., I knew what it was. I felt like Samuel who had been going to the prophet Eli, asking, "Did you call me?" I lay there with the realization that for the previous ten years God had been calling me to something new, something higher. This time He had my full attention—I was unable to move. I understood that, at least in part, this was the more that I had been asking for.

Some of the most important things that happen to us are the most difficult to explain to others, yet they are undeniably from God. The person having the encounter knows, and that's what matters most. I had been asking God to give me more of Him at any cost. I wasn't sure of the correct way to pray, nor did I understand the theology behind my request because I knew He already dwelt in me as a result of my conversion. All I knew was I was hungry for more of God. There were times I even woke myself in the night because I was asking for more in my sleep.

Here it was, 3:00 a.m., and it was my moment. But it didn't come in the way I expected—although I couldn't have told you what I expected. He had come to me on a mission. I was His target. It was a glorious experience, because it was Him. But it was not a very pleasant one. It was not gratifying in any natural sense.

At first I was embarrassed. I felt my face turn red, even though I was the only one who knew I was in that condition.

As I lay there, I had a mental picture of myself standing before my congregation, teaching from God's Word as I loved to do, but with my arms and legs flailing about as though I had serious physical and emotional problems. Then I saw myself walking down the main street of our town in front of my favorite restaurant in the same condition. I didn't know anyone who would believe that this was from God.

But then I recalled Jacob and his encounter with the angel of the Lord, where he wrestled with Him throughout the night. He limped for the rest of his life after his meeting with God. And then there was Mary, the mother of Jesus. She had an experience with God that not even her fiancé believed was true. It took a visit from an angel to help him change his mind. As a result she bore the Christ-child... and then bore a stigma for the remainder of her days as the mother of the illegitimate child. As I considered these stories something became clear: from earth's perspective the favor of God sometimes looks different than from Heaven's perspective. My request for more of God carried a price.

Tears began to soak my pillowcase as He reminded me of my prayers over the previous months, contrasting them with the scenes that had just passed through my mind. I was gripped by the realization that God wanted to make an exchange—an increased manifestation of His presence in exchange for my dignity, for I had prayed, "at any cost."

It's difficult to explain how exactly one knows the purpose for such encounters. All I can say is you just know. You know His purpose so clearly that every other reality fades into the shadows as God puts His finger on the one thing that matters to Him.

It was in this place, not knowing if I would ever function as a normal human being again, wondering if I would actually be bedridden for the rest of my life because of this overwhelming presence, that, in the midst of the tears, I came to my point of no return. I gladly yielded, crying, "More, God. More! I must have more of You at any cost! If I lose respectability and get You in the exchange, I'll gladly make that trade. Just give me more of You!"

The power surges didn't stop. They continued throughout the night, with me weeping and praying, More Lord, more, please give me more of You. Then it all stopped at 6:38 A.M., when I got out of bed completely refreshed.

This experience continued the following two nights, beginning moments after getting into bed. When they finished, I no longer thought the way I thought before. My mind had been completely transformed.

Beni Johnson

"What is going on?" was the question my friend asked me at a women's retreat.

Bill and I were pastoring a small church in the mountains of northern California. In the mid-90's when our ladies decided to have their first women's retreat. I was scared because I knew I would have to speak. It was terrifying to have to get up in front of people. I just knew that I would get up there and blank out and forget what I was going to say. Hor-

Whole Lotta Shaking

rible thoughts were going through my head. I was so afraid of everything that had anything to do with communicating publicly. But several of us ladies from the church would be speaking, and that was a relief for me.

On one of the nights when I wasn't speaking, I was sitting towards the back. I can't remember what brought the Holy Spirit into the building, but for whatever it was, I am forever grateful. I was just minding my own business and all of a sudden, something inside of my gut, my innermost being, exploded. My stomach shook inside and I began to cry.

I couldn't stop sobbing and the movement of the Holy Spirit began dismantling me from the inside out. It was like I had all this stuff closed inside, and a bomb went off and opened my spirit. When a friend came over and asked me what was going on and if it was God, I told her it was God, but I didn't know what was happening. I had never experienced God in that way before— but I have now come to know that explosion is His presence in me. Sometimes it's quite an inner explosion, and other times it shakes my physical being. I have felt it many times since that moment.

After that day, my spirit was more alive and tuned. I had always been sensitive to things around me but now things were different. I was tuning into a new dimension of God.

Shortly after this experience, my husband took me to Airport Christian Fellowship in Toronto, Canada, where a great renewal of God's love was being poured out. Bill had been before and wanted me to go and experience what was going on. I was already pretty messed up from my retreat experience, and it wouldn't take much to put me over the edge again.

Whole Lotta Shaking

One night after the meeting ended, we were headed to the back of the church and there were people laid out all over the floor laughing and having all kinds of physical manifestations. I was holding onto Bill's arm, and I noticed what looked like a very inebriated man, staggering around touching people. I had heard of this condition before and knew that this man was "drunk in the Holy Spirit."

What happened next changed my life forever, and I will always be grateful to that man for his drunkenness. He and I made eye contact, and he headed straight towards me. When he reached me, he touched me with his finger on my forearm. That was all, and that was enough. A holy current went right into me, not just on the outside of me but on the inside as well. When that current hit me, I began to shake so violently that my husband had to let go of my arm. I fell to the ground and, for the next half hour, looked like I was plugged into an electrical socket.

My husband told me later he had never seen anything like it (and has never since). I had absolutely no control over my body. I would try to stop the shaking, but it would just get worse. I knew it was God, just like at that women's retreat, but I had no idea what was happening.

My life changed that day. I came in contact with the energy of heaven. Heavenly energy is high voltage and extremely powerful. Everything that is in the way of that glory energy that is not of God will go! I had a massive deliverance. I was no longer afraid. That encounter shook all the fear right out of me. I fell madly, deeply in love with the Holy Spirit. I was a goner. Any time anybody said anything about God, Jesus or the Holy Spirit, I would start weeping and laughing at the same time.

I still have those inner movements of God's presence, those vibrations from heaven, on a regular basis. When I experience His presence like that and I move into a time of intercession, I know things will happen.

Cal Pierce

In June, 1996, I was at a meeting at Bethel Assembly of God in Redding, CA. I was on the church Board and you might say I was the most bored Board Member there has ever been. Church had become just same-old, same-old. I loved God and believed in Him, but I didn't really have a passion for much of anything.

That night, at the meeting's conclusion, Bill Johnson went around the room praying for each of us. Without warning, I felt such a tremendous jolt of the power of God that my whole body began vibrating as if an electric current was running through it and I was shaking so hard I couldn't move. This lasted for hours, with me shaking and unable to move.

When the shaking finally stopped, my life was completely changed. You might say I became "on fire" for God. I suddenly had a passion for God I'd never had before. I became interested in what had happened to John G. Lake's healing rooms and, in November, 1997 my wife Michelle and I felt drawn to Spokane, the location of Lake's original healing rooms.

We sold everything, packed up our furniture, and moved to Spokane having never been there before. We weren't sure exactly what God wanted us to do, so I decided to visit John G. Lake's grave. For over a year I returned to his grave to pray once a month.

On February 28, 1999 I started a 40 day fast. I went to Lake's gravesite to pray when I heard God say, "There is a time to pray, and a time to move."

I called in intercessors and began training up healing teams. On July 22, 1999 the Spokane Healing Rooms of John G. Lake were re-opened in the same location they had been 80 years before. The International Association of Healing Rooms now has healing rooms all across the United States and in over 50 nations.

Ellyn Davis

I've had quite a few traumatic experiences in my life, but from 2006 to 2009 were possibly the most traumatic years of my life. I had the devastating losses of coming to the end of a long-term relationship, being betrayed by a business partner I loved and deeply trusted, having my mother die after months of slow, steady decline, and having my youngest child leave home.

In the process, I lost three businesses as well as all of the money I had invested in them.

The combination of the different events affected me on every level—physically, mentally, emotionally, spiritually, and financially. I wound up physically ill and on the verge of a mental and emotional breakdown. In addition, I found myself in severe financial distress.

Whole Lotta Shaking

My chiropractor told me that stress and trauma is often stored in our tissues and I believed him because my neck, back and hip needed constant re-adjustment plus I began having intestinal problems as well as frequent unexplainable infections.

As I went through the grieving process, the forgiveness process, the inner healing process, the physical healing process as well as the process of dealing with a mountain of debt, I spent a lot of time in prayer and would often have vibrating, tingling, electrical shock, flashing light types of sensations.

Sometimes my body would shake so violently I could hardly control it. Other times I would feel like a low-voltage electrical current was running through me. The electrical tingling often centered in my head and I could actually feel that my brain was being re-wired and negative thought patterns were being disrupted and replaced by positive ones. When my body tingled or vibrated, I could sense that traumatic and negative emotions and memories were being released.

Sometimes I would see flashes of light and sometimes it would be like a net of peace with a thousand twinkling lights was enveloping me.

It took awhile, but I eventually recovered from the trauma and when I did I was a different person mentally, emotionally, and spiritually. Almost all of my physical problems were gone, my finances were headed in the right direction, and I regained my interest in life.

Whole Lotta Shaking

Note: The following two testimonies were e-mailed to Judy.

Celeste

One night in 2006, I had a dream. I was with some friends at school and we were walking down the hallway and met a man. My friends knew the man and introduced me to him. There was something very familiar about him.

When he shook my hand he pulled me close to him into a hug. My cheek touched his cheek and electricity shot through my body. I pulled back in shock and looked at his face. He was the most beautiful man I had ever seen. I felt a deep connection to him that I had never felt before. In the dream, my body began vibrating. When I woke up, I was still vibrating like something inside my core had been shocked by electricity. The vibrations lasted for about 30 minutes.

This was the first time I'd had any experience like this. I had never met anyone who had experienced anything like it either. I had only read about it in books.

I asked God what the dream was about. He said, "I gave you that dream so you would stop asking me who your husband is." I then knew that the man in my dream was my husband. The connection and the spark and the love I felt was something from another realm. From that day forward I knew who I was looking for!

I moved to Vietnam for a year to do missions and while I was there Jesus took me on bizarre love-filled journeys and told me many amazing things. But I never saw His face. I wasn't even sure if that was possible. I wanted to see his face, but I was also OK with just being with Him.

Whole Lotta Shaking

In 2008, after I returned to America, I attended a women's conference where Judy Franklin and Beni Johnson were speaking. One afternoon, Judy took all of us to heaven. She told us to ask Jesus to take us to a favorite place. Much to my surprise, I went to places in heaven I had been going with Jesus for a long time. Then Judy asked us to look at Jesus. So I asked Him to walk in front of me....and it was the man from my dream! The most beautiful man I had ever seen. My Husband! I laughed and cried! Jesus had a big smile on his face, like He had been so sneaky, but He was so kind and playful about it!

This experience changed my whole life! I had a very tangible encounter with Jesus and sometimes I can feel the vibration inside my core when I think about Him!

John

My sister, Mary Ann, was a sold-out charismatic believer who prayed for me many years, displayed a joyous salvation, and sent me some current best-selling Christian charismatic books. Having just graduated from Memphis State University in 1967, I planned a trip to Lexington, Kentucky to visit Mary Ann and her family.

I arrived on a Sunday evening, only to be asked if I would go with her to her Monday morning prayer group at their church. My sister and I are extremely close, so I reluctantly agreed to go, even though I didn't really want to.

The next morning, we all sat around in a circle in the basement of the church. I was introduced, there was some chit-chat, then they began to pray. My mind quickly drifted from the prayers, and I heard some children laughing outside the window to my right.

Suddenly, my eyes filled with the brightest, most vibrant light imaginable, and in a millisecond, I knew the reality of Jesus! I literally lost my breath and began thinking, "He's real; He really is real!" I could hardly contain myself, and tried to grasp what had happened. When the prayer meeting was over, I told Mary Ann what had happened. She was beyond herself, and we quickly left for home.

When her husband came in later that day, she asked me to share with him what had happened. He listened intently, then excused himself and went to their bedroom. Later he again joined us, and his countenance looked totally different. He too had an encounter with God and the three of us excitedly talked about the day's events.

My life was totally transformed by knowing the reality of Jesus through that bright light. The beginning journey of my faith was one of a driving desire to know the One who had saved me. The thrill of that day and those early days of pursuing Him caused me to eventually come on staff at an outreach ministry called Christ Center. This is where I met my wife, Judy. Today, I am just as excited about pursuing Jesus and extending His Kingdom, as I was the day I first saw that bright light.

Have you had an encounter with God that involved light, sound, vibrations, or electricity? We'd love to hear about it. Scan this QR code with your smartphone or go to www.heavensphysics.com/Chapter14.

Your Body is an Electromagnetic Field

You may not realize it, but each part of your body has its own resonant frequency. Because of this, military studies have identified the parts of the body most susceptible to the frequencies of vibrations in aircraft and pilots are trained to recognize when their body is being exposed to a matching vibrational frequency so their performance will not be impaired. Everything about you vibrates at a certain frequency, even your DNA.

In addition, every sense is essentially a receiver and interpreter of vibrations. Hearing receives and interprets the vibration of sound; seeing receives and interprets the vibration of light; touching and smelling and tasting all involve sensing and interpreting the vibrations of different molecules of matter.

Your whole being is an electromagnetic field and different parts of your body emit different electromagnetic vibrations.

In 1924, Willem Einthoven received a Nobel Prize for his discovery that heart electricity could be recorded with a galvanometer. In the 1970's magnetometers were developed that could measure brain fields. Now, the electrocardiogram (ECG) and electroencephalogram (EEG) are standard tools for medical diagnosis.

E.T. may have been right about us having a "heart light." Your heart is by far your strongest electromagnetic generator. It creates a magnetic field that is up to 5000 times stronger than the field generated by your brain. This strong pulsating magnetic field spreads out in front of and behind the body, and instruments are now available that can detect the field of the heart 15 feet away from the body. It is most coherent when a person is in a loving or caring state.

The HeartMath Institute has studied the exchange of heart electromagnetic energy when people touch or are in proximity and found that one person's ECG signal registered in another's EEG and elsewhere on the other person's body. They also determined that the cardiac field changes as different emotions are experienced and this field is registered physiologically by those around us.

Virtually all the tissues in the body generate electrical fields when compressed and stretched and any movement of any part of the body broadcasts a "biomagnetic" signature of that movement into the space around the body.

Sensing Magnetic Fields

Sea turtles, pigeons, honeybees, cattle, deer, monarch butterflies, and foxes are among the animals that have an incredibly useful skill we humans don't possess—or at least don't know how to access yet. They can sense the Earth's magnetic field with their bodies.

The motion of Earth's fluid core generates electric currents that produce magnetic fields which combine to create a vast magnetic field that acts as a shield against the damaging effects of solar winds. Many animals can detect the Earth's magnetic field, which reveals the direction of magnetic north, and these animals use it to orient themselves and to navigate.

Newly hatched sea turtles can not only sense magnetic north, but they can use the Earth's magnetic field to determine their longitudinal position—which is a feat that took sailors centuries to figure out how to determine.

How animals sense the magnetic field is still unknown, but scientists do know that there are magnetoreceptors in the upper beaks of migratory birds which allow the birds to sense their position, much like the turtles seem able to do.

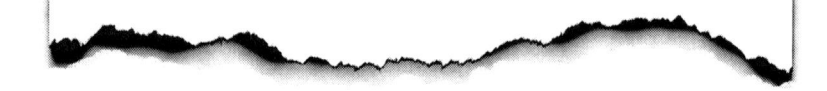

15

The Clarion Call
by Beni Johnson

In this chapter, Beni Johnson shares that God is issuing a clarion (a shrill and clear sound) calling us to venture into new realms, including realms of the vibrations of heaven.

I love to hear the sound of heaven come into a room during a time of worship. I will purposely listen for it, because when it comes, it shifts the atmosphere. When that worship leader and his team of worshippers hit the right note or play the right song, heaven comes a little closer. What a feeling that is! I practice hearing this during worship time, for it is time to train our spirit ears to hear that sound. When we practice this, we will be able to step into the moment.

God always has a reason for releasing His sound, and the result is to always bring us closer to Him. You can watch a person who is unsaved but searching for truth walk into a meeting when there is that worship sound going on. They know something is happening though they may not be able to understand it, but whatever it is, they want it.

My husband and I watched this happen once to a young woman who stood right in front of us during one of our worship times. It was obvious she wasn't saved, but she was so drawn by the music that she did what she knew to do. We watched as she began to do her hand motions and dance. We knew that what she was generating was what we call "strange fire," not a good thing. But, that's all she knew to do. It was very cold around her as well.

My husband called our lead dancer to go up on stage and dance/worship to break this strange fire. The minute our dancer took her first step, the young gal in front of us dropped to the ground. She turned to me and said, "I want to do that," speaking of our dancer and what she was doing. I knelt down and talked with her, led her to the Lord and brought some deliverance to her. The strange fire stopped and salvation came, all because of a sound that stirred someone who needed Jesus. Wow!

When you connect to the spirit realm, you make an alliance with that sound of heaven and all things move to that sound. I love the feeling that I get when I know that I have connected with God and can release heaven's sound over situations. That is when I know change is at hand.

A Sound Like a Wind

One of the most dramatic accounts in the Bible is of the day of Pentecost.

> *When the Day of Pentecost had fully come, they were all with one accord in one place. And suddenly there came a sound from heaven, as of a rushing mighty wind, and it filled the whole house where they*

were sitting. Then there appeared to them divided tongues, as of fire, and one sat upon each of them. And they were all filled with the Holy Spirit and began to speak with other tongues, as the Spirit gave them utterance. And there were dwelling in Jerusalem Jews, devout men, from every nation under heaven. And when this sound occurred, a multitude came together, and were confused, because everyone heard them speak in his own language. Then they were all amazed and marveled, saying to one another, "Look, are not all these who speak Galileans?" (Acts 2:1-7).

I would have loved being in that upper room on that day of Pentecost in Acts 2 with all of those people praying.

Look what a sound from heaven could do: first fruits and harvest! The church started that day; many were filled with the Holy Spirit and fire.; and as far as we know, it was the first of the harvest of souls. Look at verses 38 – 41 of Acts 2:

Then Peter said to them, "Repent, and let every one of you be baptized in the name of Jesus Christ for the remission of sins; and you shall receive the gift of the Holy Spirit. For the promise is to you and to your children, and to all who are afar off, as many as the Lord our God will call."

And with many other words he testified and exhorted them, saying, "Be saved from this perverse generation." Then those who gladly received his word were baptized; and that day about three thousand souls were added to them.

The Clarion Call

A little side note here, Peter for the first time realized who he was and gave his first evangelistic message that brought 3,000 souls into the Kingdom. Just think, it could have been the first time he ever preached the salvation message. Peter, the man who always seemed to open his mouth at the wrong time was now right on track.

Birds in Wales

Bill and I were invited to speak in Wales at a conference. The evening we arrived, Bill was scheduled to speak. To say the least, I was suffering from major jet lag. Bill was fine, but I was having a problem staying awake. Bill began to speak and as he reached the end of his message, the only thought in my head was how much I wanted to get to the hotel room and go to bed. At the close of the meeting, Bill had everyone stand to pray.

I was so tired, I was having a hard time paying attention to what was going on, which for me is when God seems to show up and be out of the box with what He wants to show me. Bill asked the people to pray, and, as they began praying, out of somewhere I heard an unusual sound come into the room. I had heard that particular sound before but couldn't place it. It started as the people prayed. Bill had them stop and gave them a second thing to pray about.

As the people began praying again, I heard the sound again. What in the world was that? This happened three times, and each time the people prayed that sound came. I've learned that for me, when God speaks three times about something, He is saying, "Listen, I'm wanting you to get something here." On the third time of prayer, I figured out what the sound was.

Have you ever been walking outside and come to a tree and heard hundreds of birds chattering? That was the sound that I heard, a loud noise like a whole flock of birds chirping in a tree.

Three times that happened. On the third time, while the people were still praying, Bill came down from the podium and said to me, "It sounds like birds in here. Whatever could that mean?"

Well, I was determined to find out. It was obvious that God was trying to speak. We ended the meeting and went back to the hotel. Right before I got into bed, I went to my Facebook account and typed in, "What does it mean when birds in trees are squawking?" I closed my computer and went to bed. The next morning I found some pretty funny responses to my question. But, one comment got my attention. A guy had done a study on the subject of birds in trees and the noise they make and he wrote to me that when birds make that sound they are saying things like, "This isn't your place. Get away! You can't have this."

As I read his response, I understood what the bird sounds meant. I realized that as the people were praying the night before and that sound came into the room each time they prayed, there was a spirit of prayer that was saying, "You can't have this. Get away! This is ours." Then I got this revelation of what God was saying: It is time we move in authority in our prayers over territory. It is a time of territorial praying. There were things that God wanted us to take over territorially and say to the enemy, "You cannot have this; it's not yours. Get away."

That afternoon at the conference while I spoke, I shared the whole experience and what I felt God was telling us: we were moving into new authority over things that we had been praying about and that our prayers were like that sound in the trees, territorial prayers.

At the end of the message, I had everyone in the room write down something they had been praying for on a piece of paper, then we began to stand in prayer with authority over those requests, connecting with that sound from heaven to bring an answer.

I had them use their prayer language. They raised their voices and began praying. I encouraged them to keep at it because we needed to reach the spiritual place where that bird sound came from.

I remember pacing on the stage speaking in tongues with them. I remember saying, "higher, higher, higher" and, finally, the sound came into the room. The authority was there to change the atmosphere. It was done. Now that's one good prayer meeting when you can hear and feel a sound that causes a shift in the air. Things happen and answers will come. It's a joining with heaven to bring heaven's reign.

We are in a time when we need the sound of heaven, where our prayers become one—a harmonious sound. There is nothing sweeter-sounding than some good harmonies in a song. As our prayers pick up on the harmony of heaven, we become a sweet sound across our land.

The Clarion Call

Take time to be alone and listen and wait for His sound to come to your spirit. As you deliberately shift your attention, you can physically feel Him stirring in your innermost being, changing and shifting you. The vibrations of heaven are a powerful life-changing substance. Anything is possible when you plug in.

Go to www.heavensphysics.com/chapter15 or scan this QR code on your smartphone to share your insights and spiritual experiences on topics covered in this chapter.

Human Body Frequencies

In the 1920's, Dr. Royal Rife developed a machine that applied currents of specific frequencies to the body to cure a wide range of diseases. His research demonstrated that certain frequencies can prevent the development of disease, and that others would destroy disease. In 1934, the University of Southern California appointed a Special Medical Research Committee to bring terminal cancer patients from Pasadena County Hospital to Rife's San Diego clinic for treatment. The total recovery rate using Rife's technology was 100%.

In 1992, studies conducted at Eastern State University in Cheny, Washington, determined that the average, daytime frequency of the human body is 62-68 Hz. When a person's frequency drops, the immune system is compromised and disease develops.

Another example of the importance of body frequencies for health comes from a radiologist from Sweden, Bjorn Nordenstrom. In the early 1980's he discovered that, by putting an electrode inside a tumor and running a milliamp of DC current through the electrode, he could stop the growth of the tumor and cause it to dissolve.

16

Pulling the Tomorrows of God Into Today
by Bill Johnson

All of the contributors to chapters in this book sense that God is on the verge of releasing something new on the earth and that new thing somehow involves vibrations, frequencies, energy, sound, light, and taking "quantum leaps" by faith. In this chapter, Bill Johnson shares how we already own in the present what is not yet. And, because of our inheritance in Christ, we can reach into God for what has been reserved for tomorrow and pull it into our today.

Our role in shaping the world around us through creative expression is never more at the forefront than when we joyfully learn to pull tomorrow into today. God trains us for this role whenever He speaks to us, for in doing so He is working to awaken and establish our affections for His kingdom. A people whose hearts are anchored in His world are best qualified to serve in this one. He establishes His eternal purpose in us whenever He speaks. His word comes from eternity into time, giving us a track to ride on. It connects us with eternity, causing us to affect our world through the influence of His world.

Pulling Into Today

Inheritance 101

The believer's inheritance is beyond human comprehension. To put the richness of that gift into the eternal future is to sell short the power of the cross in the present. He gave us a gift beyond comprehension because we have an assignment beyond reason. Jesus gave us all things because we would need all things to fulfill our call. He intends to fill the earth with His glory, and His glorious bride will play a role.

It is interesting to note that we have already inherited tomorrow—things to come. That makes us stewards of tomorrow in a profound way. God reveals coming events to us, and we steward the timing of those events. This amazing privilege is exemplified in Scripture and gives insight to passages that might otherwise be hard to understand.

Israel was Blinded by God

Many times throughout the Scriptures we are faced with statements and principles that challenge our understanding of God. It's never that He could be perceived as evil or untrustworthy; but He is often mysterious and unpredictable.

Such a case is found in the Gospel of John. At first glance it looks as though God has it in for Israel and that He hopes they don't repent because He doesn't want to heal them.

> *He has blinded their eyes and He hardened their heart, so that they would not see with their eyes and perceive with their heart, and be converted and I should heal them. (John 12:40)*

Pulling Into Today

Yet the whole of Scripture gives us a different picture. We know God never hardens a tender heart. It's the tender heart that receives what God is saying and doing. Wherever people have truly sought God, He has welcomed them with great mercy and grace, as He is the restorer of broken lives. But a hard heart is a different story completely, as God will harden a hard heart.

Pharaoh is probably the best example of this. The Bible says that he hardened his heart against the Lord, and did so repeatedly. So God finally hardened his heart for him, making his condition permanent. If Pharaoh would not be used as an instrument of righteousness, then God would use his evil to display His wonders. God's intent was now to use him as a chess piece for His purposes.

Israel was similarly hardened and used for God's purposes. They had watched Jesus' ministry firsthand for over 3 years. While Nazareth was the only city we know of to resist because of unbelief, the others still didn't repent even though they saw extraordinary miracles. Seeing God display His wonders has a price tag—we can no longer live (think and act) the same way we did before. Miracles display God's dominion with a clarity that is seldom seen in the rest of life. To see and not change is to bring judgment upon ourselves. Such was the case for many of the cities of Israel.

God is perfect in wisdom, and is able to use the worst that man can dish out for His glory. In His sovereignty, He chose to use this season of rejection of the gospel as the time He would add the Gentiles to the faith. This is discussed more clearly in Romans 11: 11.

Pulling Into Today

I say then, have they stumbled that they should fall? Certainly not! But through their fall, to provoke them to jealousy, salvation has come to the Gentiles.

Israel's rejection of Jesus provided the opportunity for the Gentiles to be grafted into the olive tree, the Israel of God. The entire story is a fascinating study on God's sovereign plan to save people from every tribe, tongue, and nation, but unpacking this is not the purpose of this chapter. Rather, tucked away in this wonderful story is a remarkable truth: if Israel understood what God had purposed for them within His kingdom in the last days, and if they had asked for it, God would have had to give it to them. He would have answered them even though it was NOT His correct time for that promise to be fulfilled. So He used their hardness of heart as the basis for blinding them to insure that His purposes would be accomplished on His timetable. Instead of just saying "no," He responded by hardening their already hard hearts so they would lose their ability to perceive kingdom possibilities.

The implication of the story is this—if you see it, you can have it! Perhaps it would be better to say, if God lets you see future promises, it's because He's hoping they will hook you, and cause you to hunger for those things. It is through a desperate heart that you are able to bring the fulfillment of those promises into your day.

The Purpose of Revelation

Revelation means 'to lift the veil'. It is to remove a cover over something so we can see it more clearly. It doesn't create something; it simply reveals what was already there. When God reveals coming events and promises, He is giving us access to a realm in Him. All of the promises He reveals to us will be realized in time, but the acceleration of events is largely determined by the desperation of God's people.

Our passion for Him and His promises speeds up the process of growth and development, making us qualified for the stewardship of those events sooner than had been planned.

Jesus and His mother, Mary, went to a wedding in John chapter 2. After they were there for a while, Mary noticed the wedding party was out of wine. She spoke to Jesus about their problem. Jesus' responded, "Woman, what does that have to do with us? My hour has not yet come."

Since Jesus only said and did what He picked up from His Father, He let her know that this was not the right time to reveal Himself as the miracle worker.

Mary had been pregnant with God's promises about her son for 30 years, and found it difficult to wait much longer. She turned to the servants and told them to do whatever Jesus said. Jesus, who got all His direction from His heavenly Father, now perceived that this had become the right time. Amazing! God's timing changed! What was reserved for another day (revealing Jesus as the miracle worker) was pulled into her day through her desperation.

Another time Jesus ministered to the woman at the well. She was a Samaritan. Jesus so profoundly impacted her that she was able to persuade the entire city to come and hear Him speak. They believed at first because of the woman's testimony, but ended up believing out of their personal contact with Him.

Pulling Into Today

What is important to remember is that this was not supposed to be the time for the non-Jews to hear the gospel. The disciples were not even allowed the chance to preach to them when they were commissioned in Matthew 10 , because that new focus would come after the death and resurrection of Jesus. Yet in this story, the people of the city begged Jesus to stay two more days, which He did. They pulled a privilege into their day that was reserved for another time.

The Most Profound Story

King David takes the prize for having perhaps the greatest story which illustrates this principle. His situation is hard for us to imagine—he was under the law. Only the high priest could come before the actual presence of God Whose presence dwelt upon the mercy seat, which was inside the Holy of Holies. The high priest could only come bringing a basin of blood, hoping that God would indeed accept the sacrifice and postpone the penalty of sin for one more year. If anyone other than the priest ever came into God's actual presence, that person would die. God would kill him. There certainly wasn't a careless attitude about going to church in those days.

David is known as the man after God's heart. He had a revelation of changes in their approach to God, confirmed by Nathan and Gad, the prophets who served in his court. This insight changed everything. He saw that the blood of bulls and goats did nothing to really touch the heart of God, and that He was really looking for the sacrifices of brokenness and contrition. Another radical change that would have been nearly unimaginable in that day was that every priest would be welcome into God's presence daily. And they didn't come with a basin of blood, but instead came offering sacrifices of thanksgiving and praise.

Preparations began. The musicians and singers were trained. Israel was getting herself ready for the presence of God to return to Jerusalem. Saul, Israel's former king, had little regard for the Ark of the Covenant. But David wanted God's presence more than anything. While there were initial problems, due to the fact they did not follow God's instructions for carrying the Ark of the Covenant, David eventually got his wish. He pitched a tent for the Ark and with great celebration brought the Presence into the city and placed it into the tent. According to David's directions, the priests ministered to God 24 hours a day, for decades. There were no sacrifices of animals before His presence in this tent. It was 100% worship.

It's important to note two things: One, what they did was forbidden by the law they lived under. And two, they were given a sneak preview of New Testament church life. Because of the blood of Jesus, each believer has access to the presence of God to minister to Him with thanksgiving, praise, and worship.

David was primarily a worshiper. As a young man he no doubt learned much about the presence and heart of God. He tasted of a lifestyle that was reserved for New Testament believers, yet hungered for that in his day. His hunger for what he saw became so strong that God let him have something in his day that was reserved for another day.

Pulling Into Today

Our Greatest Challenge

If it's true that the promises of restored cities and healed nations are actually millennium promises . . . and if the promise of God's glory being manifest all over the earth is far off into the future . . . and if in fact the people of God will not reach a place of true maturity, living like one mature man—then I must ask the question—is there anyone hungry enough for what He has shown us in the Scriptures that we will pull into our day something that is reserved for another? Is there anyone willing to lay themselves down to bring more of God's promises across another great divide?

If you can see God's coming future promises, and He hasn't blinded your eyes to His intent, then He is hoping to hook you into the role of calling "into being that which does not exist." It is the role of the desperate heart of faith. We have the opportunity to affect the direction and flow of history through our prayers and intercessions. This is where we take hold of the future. This is why He wants to show us, "things to come." The future is now, and it belongs to us.

It's a New Day . . . Dreamers, Let's Gather

God doesn't reveal coming events to make us strategists. He shows us the future to make us dissatisfied because hungry people move the resources of Heaven like no one else possibly could. It's the real reason the rich have such a hard time entering the kingdom—there's so little hunger for what is real, what is unseen—their desperation has been numbed by an abundance of the inferior.

Pulling Into Today

We are in a race. It's a race between what is and what could be. We are uniquely positioned with the richest inheritance of all time. It has been accumulating through several thousand years of man encountering God, and God encountering man. The righteous dead are watching. They fill the heavenly stands, and have been given the name, "cloud of witnesses." They realize that in a relay race, each runner receives a prize according to how the last runner finishes. They invested in us for this final leg of the race, and are now waiting to see what we will do with what we've been given.

If you can see God's coming future promises, and He hasn't blinded your eyes to His intent, then He is hoping to hook you into the role of calling "into being that which does not exist."

We've been given the capacity to dream and, more importantly, to dream with God. His language continues to be unveiled, His heart is being imparted, and permission has been given to try to exaggerate His goodness. We have been given the right to surpass the accomplishments of previous generations using creativity through wisdom to solve the issues facing mankind. Their ceiling is our floor. This is our time to run.

Only Children are Ready

I remember when I was a child and my parents would have guests come over to our house to visit. It was always excit-

Pulling Into Today

ing to be a part of the food and the fun. But it was painful to have to go to bed while they were still there, sitting in our living room, talking and having fun. The laughter that echoed back into my room was just torture. It was impossible for me to sleep in that atmosphere.

Sometimes, when I couldn't take it any longer, I would sneak quietly into the hallway, just to listen. I didn't want to miss anything. If my parents caught me they usually sent me back to bed. But there were a few times when they thought my curiosity was humorous enough to let me come out to be with them just a little longer. The risk was worth it!

I'm in the hallway again. And the thought of missing something that could have been the experience of my generation is pure torture. I can't possibly sleep in this atmosphere, because if I do, I know I'll miss the reason for which I was born.

This chapter is excerpted and reproduced by permission of Destiny Image Publishers from Bill Johnson's book **Dreaming With God***, ©2006, Destiny Image Publishers.*

Go to www.heavensphysics.com/chapter16 or scan this QR code on your smartphone to share your insights and spiritual experiences on topics covered in this chapter.

About the Authors

Authors

Judy Franklin. Judy is administrative assistant to Bill Johnson, a conference speaker, and author of the book *Experiencing the Heavenly Realm*. Her experiences with God have made her a bridge for many into the invisible realm. She has a heart for showing others how to have an intimate relationship with God. Visit Judy's website at www.experiencingheaven.com.

Ellyn Davis. Although her B.S. and graduate studies are in scientific fields, after a brief career in research at Emory University in Atlanta, Ellyn took time off to raise a family and develop several businesses. In 1989, Ellyn founded the Elijah Company which eventually became one of the world's largest suppliers of Christian home education materials. Ellyn has written three bestselling books for Christian home schoolers and has been a contributor to leading home schooling magazines as well as a sought-after speaker. She is also a publisher and editor. Over the past ten years Ellyn has had a desire to bridge the gap between Christianity and the discoveries of

About the Authors

quantum physics as well as discover God truths hidden in quantum mysticism and the New Age. Visit her website at www.raggedreason.com.

Contributors

Note: *All contributor chapters were adapted and edited by Ellyn Davis.*

Bob Jones. Bob Jones is known as a contemporary prophet with a great love for the Lord Jesus and His truth. His prophesies have spanned over four decades. Like Daniel, who functioned at an incredible level of insight, Bob has often told leaders their dreams and experiences, as well as the interpretation. After a death experience in 1975, God sent Bob back to minister to church leadership and equip the saints with understanding of the spiritual gifts. God promised Bob that he would see the beginning of one billion souls coming into the kingdom in one great wave of the end time harvest. Visit Bob's website at www.bobjones.org. Bob's chapter is excerpted from an audio interview.

Bill Johnson. Bill is a fifth generation pastor with a rich heritage in the things of the Spirit. He is Senior Pastor of Bethel Church in Redding, CA and has written numerous best-selling books including the popular *When Heaven Invades Earth*. Along with his wife Beni, Bill serves a growing number of churches that have partnered for revival. This apostolic network has crossed denominational lines in building relationships that enable church leaders to walk in both

About the Authors

purity and power. Visit Bill's website at www.bjm.org. Bill's chapter on inheritance was adapted from his audio series *Spiritual Inheritance*. His chapter on "Pulling Into Today" was adapted from his book *Dreaming With God*.

Beni Johnson. Beni and her husband Bill are senior pastors at Bethel Church in Redding, CA. Beni has a call to intercession that is an integral part of the Bethel Church mission. She is in charge of the Bethel's Prayer House, ministry teams and the intercessors. The Lord has given her a heart for broken people of all ages. Her insight into strategies for prayer and her involvement in prayer networks have helped to bring the much-needed breakthrough in Bethel's ministry. She is the author of the best-selling book *The Happy Intercessor* and her approach to intercession makes supernatural connections with the Lord accessible to all.

Jonathan Welton. A fifth generation believer, Jonathan Welton is propelled by a powerful Christian heritage. Exhibiting extraordinary wisdom as a teacher, he helps individuals discover fresh experiences of kingdom realities. Carrying a revelatory forerunner anointing, he trains and equips believers to use their spiritual senses to see in the unseen realm. Jonathan has earned two Masters Degrees, one in Biblical Studies and the other in Practical Ministry, as well as the National Herald of Christ Award. Jonathan's first book, *The School of the Seers: A Practical Guide on How to See into the Unseen* released in 2009, is receiving world-wide attention. Visit Jonathan's website at www.jonathanwelton.com. Jonathan's chapter was excerpted from his book *Normal Christianity*.

About the Authors

Ray Hughes. Ray Hughes, founder of Selah Ministries, has been in full time ministry for 40 years. He received his Doctorate of Divinity in 1996. He travels in the U.S. and internationally as a speaker, author, storyteller, singer/songwriter and musicologist. In addition to his research and teaching expertise, Ray is recognized internationally as a clear prophetic voice. Visit Ray's website at www.selahministries.com. Ray's chapter is excerpted from his book *Sound of Heaven, Symphony of Earth*.

Larry Randolph. Larry Randolph comes from a long line of preachers and began his own ministry when he was 5 years old. At age 21 he had a dramatic encounter with the Holy Spirit which launched him into a global prophetic ministry. Larry has been deeply involved in various renewal outpourings since the 1960's and is the author of the widely acclaimed books, *User Friendly Prophecy* and *Spirit Talk*. Visit Larry's website at www.larryrandolph.com. Larry's chapter is excerpted from an audio interview.

Dan McCollam. After serving as a worship leader for 20 years and releasing kingdom worshippers locally, regionally and globally on countless mission trips to nations around the world, Dan became heart-sick over the Westernization of worship in the majority of churches in which he ministered. Indigenous sounds had often been labeled sinful by church leadership. Since the sounds of every tribe and nation are heard in heaven, becoming an agent in restoring the stolen authentic expressions of worship became a driving passion,

About the Authors

and Sounds of the Nations was born. As director of Sounds of the Nations and the Institute for Worship Arts Resources (iWAR) Dan trains indigenous peoples to write and record worship songs using their own ethnic sounds, styles, languages and instruments. Dan's chapter was excerpted from his manuscript *God Vibrations*.

Cal Pierce. After a transforming encounter with the Lord in 1996, Cal became passionate about restoring John G. Lake's healing ministry and spent the next few years praying for direction and insight, In 1999 he re-established Lake's healing rooms on the original site. Since that time the healing rooms affiliated with Pierce's International Healing Rooms have been founded across the United States as well as in over 50 different countries. Learn more at www.healingrooms.com. Cal's chapter is excerpted from an audio interview.

David Van Koevering. David Van Koevering is a writer, minister, motivational speaker, quantum physicist and inventor. His current teachings, "The Physics of Worship" and "The Science of God Sounds" are changing lives worldwide. His life's work has demonstrated his gifts as a visionary, technologist, futurist and inventor. He is respected internationally for his 30-year contribution to the development and marketing of advanced technology that has forever changed the music industry. His gift is the insight to see, and by this observation to cause, and then define and communicate what he sees to others. Visit his website at www.elsewhen.com. David's chapter was adapted from his article "Keys to Taking Your Quantum Leap."

Recommended Reading

Dreaming With God by Bill Johnson. Copyright 2006, Destiny Image Publishers

Experiencing the Heavenly Realm by Judy Franklin. Copyright 2011, Destiny Image Publishers

Normal Christianity by Jonathan Welton. Copyright 2011, Destiny Image Publishers

Quantum Glory by Phil Mason. Copyright 2010, New Earth Tribe Publications

Science and the New Age Challenge by Ernest Lucas. Copyright 1996, Inter-Varsity Press Apollos

Sound of Heaven, Symphony of Earth by Ray Hughes. Copyright 2011, BT Johnson Publishing

Spirit Talk by Larry Randolph. Copyright 2005, Morningstar Publications

The Happy Intercessor by Beni Johnson. Copyright 2009, Destiny Image Publishers

The God Theory: Universes, Zero-Point Fields, and What's Behind It All by Bernard Haisch. Copyright 2009, Weiser Books

Contact the Authors

Judy's e-mail for speaking: Judy@heavensphysics.com
Ellyn's e-mail for speaking: Ellyn@heavensphysics.com

Heaven's Physics
c/o Ellyn Davis
P. O. Box 494014
Redding, CA 96049-4014
www.heavensphysics.com

For since the creation of the world His invisible attributes are clearly seen, being understood by the things that are made, even His eternal power and Godhead....
—Romans 1: 20